HOW TO COPE
WITH
DEPRESSION

HOW TO COPE WITH DEPRESSION

A Complete Guide for You
and Your Family

J. Raymond DePaulo, Jr., M.D.,
and
Keith Russell Ablow, M.D.

McGRAW-HILL PUBLISHING COMPANY

New York   St. Louis   San Francisco   Bogotá
Hamburg   Madrid   Mexico   Milan
Montreal   Paris   São Paulo   Tokyo   Toronto

1 2 3 4 5 6 7 8 9 DOC DOC 8 9 2 1 0 9

ISBN 0-07-016409-6

LIBRARY OF CONGRESS CATALOGING-IN-PUBLICATION DATA

DePaulo, J. Raymond, Jr., M.D.
  Coping with depression.
  Bibliography: p.
  Includes index.
  1. Depression, Mental—Popular works.   2. Manic-depressive psychoses—Popular works.   I. Ablow, Keith Russell.   II. Title.
  RC537.D415   1989   616.85′27   89-2317
  ISBN 0-07-016409-6

Book design by Eve L. Kirch

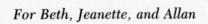

For Beth, Jeanette, and Allan

Contents

Foreword

The assumption that we all share a common propensity to respond to life's misfortunes in the same way often lies unacknowledged behind psychiatric explanations of misery and sadness. The intriguing result of this unacknowledged idea is the reflexive search for a provocative misfortune whenever a patient with a miserable state of mind appears. It is an easy, natural, indeed kindly intended, process of thought with a clear prescription. *All* depression, it says, is in some way a response to isolation or loss and thus is a form of loneliness or grief—masked and modified perhaps by personal particulars, as Freud suggested in "Mourning and Melancholia"—but ultimately it is a comprehensive response inherent to mankind. Treatment, therefore, is an amalgam of support during the distress period, illumination about the losses, and persuasion to see the losses as nondevastating and in some situations even inevitable—a process of working through the feeling state to a new personal synthesis of self-awareness and emotional control.

This entire logical path just may be the most dangerous half-truth in the psychiatric discipline. Certainly all of us are, in some situations, vulnerable to identical feelings. Certainly there are

losses in life, and many of them are "in the mind of the beholder."
But *all* the moods of misery that provoke clinical attention do not
come from these losses. Moods, like thoughts, have many sources,
and the assumption that these varied sources can be reduced to
one is seriously misleading.

I became most aware of how treacherous half-truths can be
when I was working with resident psychiatrists in the care of
elderly depressed patients. Often we would speak of the "losses
accompanying old age"—losses of vigor, social authority, and
friends—and of how these losses made somehow natural the depressive states of our patients. I remember to this day how one
of our number—quick at noting overcommitments to any idea—
broke our reverie by pointing out that most old people are not
depressed, that most of them overcome their losses without the
help of psychiatrists, and that perhaps our explanation of depressions as part of the "fellowship of old age" was a misguided sen-
timent. In fact, it was worse than a mistake, it was a blunder,
because it hindered a search for active treatment all in the name
of acceptance of some bittersweet vision of old age.

We might better, he continued, begin in exactly the opposite
way, presuming, since most elderly people cope perfectly well
with their life circumstances, that the appearance of a disabling
depression demanded an explanation beyond some metaphor of
common misfortunes and common sentiments of the aged. These
alternative explanations not only could change our therapeutics,
promoting the inclusion of medical and pharmacological treatments, but also would invigorate research into differentiating the
depressive states of the elderly—an exercise that had been hindered by the smooth mixture of fact and fiction that had seemed
so satisfactory.

I recount this incident in part because it is a choice example
of how counterinterpretations lead to progress in any field and
how their genesis requires both an extensive experience with a
subject matter and an ongoing interactive conversation among
participants. I also hold it close because its conclusion has a
powerful generality: Life is a predicament. Plenty of things go

wrong—things that happen and grieve us, things that we do and regret. But misery is far from universal. When it appears, we should beware of quick, tidy explanations, reinforced by author-itative assumptions about the "life cycle" and human nature. We should give heed to the possibility that alternative explanations may be obscured by a romantic rush to judgment about adoles-cence, "midlife," or old age.

It is this balance of experience and explanations of depression that this book provides. It is thus like a progressive clinical con-versation. It organizes its depictions of depressed patients in a way that illuminates the distinguishing features that prompt par-ticular interpretations; then it gives a lively account of the practical consequences that emerge when one or several of these explan-atory themes are woven into a clinical context.

The authors kindly suggest that they have been influenced by my teaching and that of my colleague Dr. Phillip Slavney at Johns Hopkins and by our monograph *The Perspectives of Psychiatry.* They have certainly advanced beyond our work, providing con-crete examples and practical everyday prescriptions strengthening our argument that it is part of the very nature of the psychiatric enterprise to have several paths of explanation, each of which is a logical mode of reasoning. Each may illuminate some aspect of a problem but can, if not appreciated for its limits, inhibit an open dialogue about alternatives.

Depression, depicted in this book in a variety of forms, is an ideal subject for this argument. Examples of that most common complaint help doctors, nurses, social workers, and students ap-preciate the differences that lie hidden under the common term "depression" and understand what these differences imply for treatment, prediction, and further research. The concepts in *The Perspectives of Psychiatry* have been firmly fixed in the particulars of clinical experience by this text.

I believe that this book is for anyone who has ever puzzled over the problems of depression either as a professional in psy-chiatric service or as a friend or relative of a depressed person. I think that it will help its readers in many ways, but particularly by enhancing what often is a stifled conversation between parties involved in supporting patients through a course of treatment. It should replace unquestioned authority by clarifying contemporary presumptions about what we know and how we know it. It thus should open these presumptions to alternative paths of exploration to be discussed in clinical situations and implemented in research.

I am particularly hopeful that the parents of young depressed people will read this book, because I fear that in the contemporary era they, more than any others, are cut out of the conversations on cause and treatment for reasons that will not bear close scrutiny. Yet they are often the best sources of information about the patient, the natural ready providers of care and protection during recovery, and the ones who must live with the consequences if treatment fails. They have a real stake in helping to get the correct story into the therapeutic context. If we psychiatrists arm them with information and welcome an open dialogue in the course of our assessment and treatment, all will benefit.

In fact, I long for and anticipate a time when the dialogues of patients' relatives and psychiatric professionals will be as open and mutually supportive as they can be in medical disorders where explanations and treatments have achieved public consensus. This book could hasten that day by both the information it purveys and the stance it takes about patienthood.

PAUL R. McHUGH, M.D.,
Psychiatrist-in-Chief, The Johns Hopkins Hospital
Henry Phipps Professor and Director,
Department of Psychiatry,
The Johns Hopkins University School of Medicine

Preface

I have a great deal to tell you—what a bad winter I have had; how a complete nervous collapse, with an onslaught of terrifying thoughts in its train, brought me to the verge of despair, but that the prospect is pleasanter now, and that music, too, is beginning again to sound within me, and I hope soon to be quite restored.
　　　　　—Robert Schumann, composer,
　　　　　　in a letter to Felix Mendelssohn (1845)

You already know something about depression. You understand what a friend or family member means when he or she says, "I'm down in the dumps," or "I have no energy." You understand because you remember the times when you yourself were sad. Depression is, in this sense, a normal emotion.

It is harder to know that severe mood disturbances are actually diseases directly caused by brain dysfunction. They can result in extreme changes in a person's self-image, mental and physical energy, sex life, appetite, and ability to sleep. They sometimes end in suicide. Psychiatry is determined to do a better job of teaching Americans to understand that clinical depression and manic-depressive disorder are diseases with specific signs and symptoms, to recognize these serious disorders in themselves and their loved ones, and to seek the treatments that can conquer them. Today's treatments are very successful for 80 percent of the individuals afflicted with depressive and manic-depressive disorders. Ironically, only 20 percent ever receive these treatments.

We hope this book will fill the information gap and the comprehension gap. It addresses the origins of depression and manic-depressive disorder, the importance of reliable diagnosis, the positive treatments offered by psychiatry (as well as their limitations), and the important research efforts that offer hope for the future. Unique and instructive case histories of patients seen at the Johns Hopkins Hospital bring the ideas we present to life.

Depression and manic-depressive disorder are complicated conditions requiring the vision of more than one school of psychiatric thought. This book builds on the foundation provided by the four perspectives of psychiatry described by Dr. Paul McHugh, chairman of the Department of Psychiatry, and Dr. Phillip Slavney, director of Psychiatry Residency Training, at The Johns Hopkins University School of Medicine. It examines manic and depressive conditions as diseases, as manifestations of personality, as abnormal behaviors, and as understandable chapters in an individual's entire life story.

While we conclude that the most powerful and useful way to understand severe depression and manic-depressive disorder is to recognize them as diseases, we demonstrate that all four perspectives are necessary parts of a complete appreciation of the patient.

We have written this book not only for those being treated for depression (or mania) but also for those who may need such treatment and for the families and friends of both groups. We also hope that this book will find its way to students, public health officials, nurses, psychologists, social workers, and other health professionals who might derive benefit from its chapters. With 4 million Americans currently suffering from depression and manic-depressive illness, these diseases are everyone's concern.

Finally, we want to convey a sense of hope based on our strong conviction that depression and its related disorders can be understood, treated, and surmounted. Our own experiences with research and treatment give us every reason for optimism.

Acknowledgments

Our teachers, Paul McHugh, M.D., and Phillip Slavney, M.D., through their books *The Perspectives of Psychiatry* and *The Polarities of Psychiatry*, their guidance, and their personal reviews of our work, have been enormously helpful. Equally so have been our patients and their families, whose courage in the face of affective illness provided much of the inspiration for this book. Their comments on what information we most needed to cover was invaluable.

We would like to thank our agents: Michael Powers, whose untimely death takes from us a trusted professional and valued friend, enthusiastically guided our manuscript through several revisions and receptions. Special thanks are also due Betsy Nolan, whose sure hand and bright smile shepherded our words and bolstered our spirits.

Our colleagues have helped shape the ideas and skills we bring to our writing. They include Dr. Elsa Correa, Dr. Sylvia Simpson, Dr. Andrew Feinberg, Dr. Paramjit Joshi, Dr. John Lipsey, Dr. Carol Nadelson, Dr. Henry Seidel, Dr. Art Ulene, Dr. Lawrence Grouse, and Drs. Marshal and Susan Folstein.

We are also grateful to Dr. Douglas Lind and Marie Killilea, who contributed their perspective and time in reviewing parts of the manuscript, and to Ms. Gail Marsh, who typed the manuscript many times over. Several members of the Depression and Related Affective Disorders Association (DRADA) reviewed various versions of the manuscript and helped create a special environment for this project. We thank Dee and Ted Peck, Edgar Smith, and Sallie Mink.

Lastly, our families (Beth, Marianne, and Maggie DePaulo and Jeanette, Allan, and Karen Ablow), together with Deborah Small, encouraged and reviewed our work and have been tolerant of the demands, in time and energy, of our writing.

PART ONE

DEPRESSION: WHAT WE KNOW

Knowledge is power.
—Francis Bacon,
Meditationes Sacrae (1597)

CHAPTER

Defining Depression and Manic-Depressive Illness

What can we reason but from what we know?
—Alexander Pope,
"An Essay on Man" (1771)

A physician feels his mood slip to black and begins to think that leaving the house is a terrible effort. A football coach hangs himself. A college student begins staying up until five in the morning, spends her savings on a shopping spree, and begins sleeping with a string of men she hardly knows. What could the three have in common?

The answer is *affective disorders* (roughly translated, disturbances of mood) that color one's entire outlook on life. Affective disorders range from destabilizing to devastating. The two most severe varieties are major depression and manic-depressive illness.

Major depression is more than the low feeling you experience before your morning cup of coffee or after your alma mater loses one on the gridiron. It is an illness with specific *signs* (characteristics a physician observes) and *symptoms* (complaints a patient reports).

The hallmarks of major depression are persistent low mood, lowered self-attitude, and decreased mental and physical energy.

3

The disorder leads to a loss of interest in the activities that once brought pleasure. Tearfulness is common, but so is a sense of deadened emotions that can prevent "normal" crying or sadness. Depressed individuals have a particularly negative view of themselves: They may feel worthless or, worse yet, may see themselves as bad people and blame themselves for events over which they had no control. Self-confidence as well as self-esteem suffer, and victims may become quite anxious, convinced that something terrible is about to occur. *Vital sense* (mental and physical energy and efficiency) is low. Thinking may become slow, and decision making difficult. The reasoning processes of some depressed individuals become so disordered that these people may develop delusions, becoming unshakably attached to false beliefs. A depressed person may become convinced, for example, that he or she is personally responsible for all the suffering in the world. Hallucinations, in which one hears voices or sees things that are not really there, sometimes occur. Most dangerous, depressed people often brood over death and may take their own lives.

More than the mental experiences of depressed individuals seem to be disturbed. Depressed people frequently complain of bodily symptoms as well. They are often plagued by fatigue; one of our patients complained that opening her mail seemed an exhausting endeavor. They may be troubled by slowed speech or movement or, more rarely, by increased movement and restlessness. Another common problem is decreased sexual drive. Changes in appetite for food occur; decreased appetite and weight loss are the rule, but sometimes increased appetite and weight gain are the problem. Depressed people may have difficulty falling asleep or staying asleep, often waking too early in the morning. A smaller number of depressed individuals seem to sleep too much. Some patients complain of dry mouth, nausea, or changes in bowel habits (constipation is common). They sometimes report that pains travel from one place in the body to another.

A major feature of this group of disorders is the tendency toward recurrences and remissions. Of the people who experience major depression, perhaps a third go through only one episode and never have a serious recurrence. Others may suffer episodes of major depression again and again, with as long as several years between episodes. Some remain chronically depressed for years at a stretch. Still others find themselves on a roller coaster of mood swings, a condition known as *rapid cycling*.

Mania, the very highest point on the roller coaster, is the mirror image of depression. It is marked by an elevated or irritable mood and by greatly increased activity. As in depression, there are persistent changes in mood, self-attitude, and vital sense. Here, however, they all go up rather than down. People suffering from mania may seem to talk ceaselessly and may feel that their thoughts are racing through their minds. They may need much less sleep than usual.

Whereas depressed people often have very low self-esteem, manic people have inflated self-images; they feel like they're on top of the world. They may experience delusions of having special powers or famous friends, or they may hallucinate that God is speaking directly to them. The increased energy and feelings of power and infallibility that manic people experience often lead them to engage in activities that they would otherwise avoid— activities that have a high potential for painful consequences. Buying sprees, ill-advised business ventures, sexual indiscretions, and reckless driving are all common.

Those suffering from manic-depressive illness, then, alternate between depression and mania. While an episode of mania may be followed immediately by an episode of depression (or vice versa), the episodes can be more widely spaced, and many months or even years can intervene. Rarely do we see patients who cycle from one state to the other every twenty-four hours.

If it seems that we've been talking about you or someone you know as we've defined major depression and manic-depressive illness, don't be surprised. Major depression and manic-depressive illness are common and can strike anyone—male or female, black or white, highly educated or illiterate, young or old, rich or poor.

You're Not Alone

Mood states resembling major depression and manic-depressive illness are not new. Intense highs and equal lows have been described in the Old Testament and in characters from early Western literature. Shakespeare's Hamlet delivers the following famous soliloquy on suicide:

> *To be, or not to be: that is the question:*
> *Whether 'tis nobler in the mind to suffer*
> *The slings and arrows of outrageous fortune,*
> *Or to take arms against a sea of troubles,*
> *And by opposing end them? To die: to sleep . . .*

In more recent times, political leaders have apparently been victims of affective disorders. Abraham Lincoln is believed by some to have suffered from depressive illness during his presidency. Theodore Roosevelt and Winston Churchill showed some evidence of manic or depressed periods. In 1972, Senator Thomas Eagleton made headlines when his vice presidential candidacy was undermined by public reaction to the electroconvulsive, or "shock," therapy he had once received for a severe depression.

A long line of men and women in the arts have spoken of nearly incapacitating problems with mood. Gustav Mahler, the great composer, described his mood swings eloquently in a letter to a childhood friend:

> Much has happened within me since my last letter; I cannot describe it. Only this: I have become a different person. I don't know whether this new person is better, he certainly is not happier. The fires of a supreme zest for living and the most gnawing desire for death alternate in my heart, sometimes in the course of a single hour. I know only one thing: I cannot go on like this!

Virginia Woolf, the novelist, critic, and essayist, wrote clearly of her struggle to comprehend and overcome the depression that eventually led her to suicide:

It strikes me—what are these sudden fits of complete exhaustion? I come in here to write; can't even finish a sentence; and am pulled under; now is this some odd effort; the subconscious pulling me down into her? I've been reading Faber on Newman; compared his account of a nervous breakdown; the refusal of some part of the mechanism; is that what happens to me? Not quite. Because I'm not evading anything. I long to write *The Pargiters*. No. I think the effort to live in two spheres: the novel and life; is a strain. . . . To have to behave with circumspection and decision to strangers wrenches me into another region; hence the collapse.

Major depression and manic-depressive illness are among the nation's most serious health problems. The economic cost of affective disorders is enormous. Loss of work productivity, permanent disability, depression-related alcohol and drug abuse, and the actual costs of treatment contribute to the estimated $16 billion annual price tag of depression in the United States.

The human costs are even greater. About 10 percent of Americans will experience an episode of major depression at some time during their lives. Approximately 2 percent of the nation's adolescents and adults (over 4 million people) are suffering from a depressive disorder today. After their first episode, about 70 percent can expect to face major depression again. The median number of recurrences during a lifetime is four.

No one is immune. Major depression and manic-depressive illness are common in men, women, adolescents, and even children. While women have been thought to be two times more likely than men to experience an episode of depression, recent data suggest that the rates are nearly equal. Women, however, are several times more likely to seek or accept treatment.

Hold On to That Towel

This book begins with the basics (i.e., clinical features and causes) of affective disorders so that people suffering from these illnesses, as well as their families and friends, can use the knowledge we present to better understand their illnesses and to get professional help to conquer them. We believe that knowledge really is power.

We also want to share at least a little bit of the excitement we feel about the future. People suffering from affective disorders today can benefit from treatment that offers more help than ever before. Together, we can harness our current knowledge to bring hope into lives disrupted by these disorders. Patients, families, physicians, and public health workers dealing with depression have, by describing their experiences, also defined the great challenge of the next decade. So, if you're about to throw in the towel, hold on. The best is yet to come.

CHAPTER

Other Mood Matters

A lifetime of happiness! No man alive could bear it: It would be hell on earth.
—George Bernard Shaw,
Man and Superman, Act I (1903)

More on Mania

Perhaps as many as half of the people who experience serious depressions also have episodes of mania. As we explained in Chapter 1, mania is a mood disorder in which patients have too much, rather than too little, energy. The energy is accompanied by extreme happiness or irritability and can be directed into irrational and dangerous activities. These may not seem unreasonable to the affected person because he or she often has an unrealistic sense of self-importance, self-confidence, and mental speed and accuracy. The range of severity of manic symptoms is quite wide. Mild mania (called *hypomania*) may not be recognized as a problem, even by those closest to the affected person. In its mildest forms, in fact, hypomania may even enhance the performance of tasks that call for high energy and require little attention to detail. When severe, however, mania causes impairments in judgment that often lead to disability and require hospitalization for treatment.

Manic persons may, for example, attempt the impossible without sufficient regard for the consequences. Several manic individuals have had the delusion that they were able to fly and have leaped from windows with catastrophic, sometimes fatal, outcomes. Others have risked financial security by making exorbitant purchases, jumping into ill-advised investments, or even giving their money away to strangers.

The overconfidence in mania can make a person gullible at one extreme or quite persuasive at the other. One of our patients was able to obtain an unsecured $600,000 bank loan on the basis of his powerful presentation at the bank. Thankfully, the money had not been lost when his family got him to the hospital for treatment.

Inflated self-esteem may even lead an individual to the delusional idea that he or she is very powerful, very important, or infallible. At one time we were caring for four male patients with mania, each of whom entered the hospital convinced that he was Jesus Christ. Less dramatic grandiose ideas are very common.

The relationships of a manic person with others can become markedly impaired. Even mild degrees of mania may be reflected by quick wit that sometimes goes too far. Gregariousness can become overwhelming and self-confidence can become overbearing.

In more intense mania, speech is rapid and pressured (the words spill out without a break), and discourse jumps wildly from topic to topic. One manic patient described his motivation for buying a record album of Beethoven's music by saying, "I saw a man in the store with a cup of coffee." Later, he filled in the association by sharing his thoughts in rapid succession: "Coffee came from South America"; "Many Nazis went to South America after World War II"; "Nazis were from Germany"; "Beethoven was also from Germany."

Manic individuals tend to make demands rather than requests, and they can become quite hostile when their judgment is questioned by friends or relatives. Often it is apparent to everyone except the manic person, however, that he or she is showing severely impaired reasoning. If the ill person continues to make one bad judgment after another, family members, friends, and business associates can be left with a lingering loss of confidence even after the person has recovered. Moreover, some emotional injuries inflicted in the manic state (e.g., on a spouse) may cause irreparable damage to the emotional bonds of the relationship.

The complex connection between mania and depression can be seen when mania alternates with depression in a predictable, clockwork fashion (see Jonathan's story, Chapter 15). The connection is also apparent when one considers that drugs used to treat depression (*antidepressants*) can precipitate mania and that drugs used to treat mania (*neuroleptics*) can hasten the symptoms of depression.

Mixed States

A *mixed affective disorder* is one in which symptoms of depression and mania coexist. Mixed states were first described in a turn-of-the-century textbook by the great psychiatrist Emil Kraepelin. "Very often," he wrote, "we meet temporarily with states which do not exactly correspond either to manic excitement or to depression, but represent a mixture of morbid symptoms of both."

The two most common mixed states are dysphoric (unhappy) mania and exalted depression. In *dysphoric mania*, individuals have very high energy levels, racing thoughts, and pressured speech. Rather than being in an elated mood, however, they report being irritable, fearful, or unhappy. *Exalted depression* is also characterized by depressed mood, but this time in the company of grandiose delusions. One of our patients, for example, believed that she was a prophet who was condemned for having failed to save souls with her great prophetic powers.

These unusual states can confuse psychiatrists trying to make clear diagnoses. Mixed affective disorders are often mistaken, in fact, for schizophrenia. Even with correct diagnosis, mixed states tend to be more persistent and difficult to treat than either pure depression or mania. Enormous problems in interpersonal relationships result, as an overriding irritability often obscures the underlying depressed mood.

Not Quite Manic-Depressive Illness

When groups of symptoms like those of mania or depression are somewhat less severe, they are classified differently and given different names. One of these, *cyclothymic disorder* (cyclothymia), denotes people who regularly swing from a mildly elevated mood to a mildly low mood and back. Another, called *dysthymic disorder* (dysthymia), describes people with chronic mild depression. For either condition to be diagnosed, it must have been present for two years or more.

As with depression and mania, diagnosing dysthymia and cyclothymia requires more symptoms than simply a change in mood. There must also be associated features such as a change in self-confidence (decreased or inflated) or a change in vital sense.

Some people who are diagnosed as having dysthymia or cyclothymia probably have chronically pessimistic or "moody" temperaments unrelated to affective illness. Others diagnosed as dysthymic or cyclothymic suffer with less intense forms of true major depression or manic-depressive illness. This is suggested by the fact that they tend to have family members with clear-cut major depression and mania. It is also supported by their own past histories of major depressive episodes and, often, by good responses to antidepressants or lithium (see Chapter 19).

Completing the Portrait

Not all people with heart disease have had heart attacks. Some have abnormal rhythms, heart murmurs, or heart failure; others have related conditions like angina or palpitations. It should be clear that affective disorders are no different. Depression is not the only serious disorder, nor is it the only one benefiting from the pace of discovery in psychiatry. Research, in fact, continues to reveal the common themes behind problems that seem as unrelated as premenstrual syndrome and pathological gambling.

If you have seen in the preceding chapters only isolated brushstrokes of yourself or a loved one, the pages that follow may sharpen the portrait. We paint these pictures with the belief that knowledge about each problem sheds light on the others.

CHAPTER

Recognizing Depression and Mania

In a real dark night of the soul, it is always three o'clock in the morning.

—F.Scott Fitzgerald,
The Crack-Up (1945)

Although we would all like to be able to recognize depressive or manic episodes when they occur in ourselves, our family members, or our friends, it is often difficult to do so. Diagnosis always requires a professional clinical assessment.

People at risk for affective disorders, along with their friends and family members, can, however, stay alert for signs of the conditions. The central question one must answer is whether the impaired or suffering person is experiencing a persistent change of mood, self-attitude (self-esteem or self-confidence), and vital sense. These symptoms, often well hidden, may be most apparent in behavioral changes—for example, stopping work or working ceaselessly—that take place when the individual is depressed or manic.

There can also be changes in sleep, appetite, and libido, as well as speed of movement. In the most severe episodes, delusions or hallucinations can occur. Any of these should strengthen one's suspicion that an affective disorder is present.

It is important to seek help from a psychiatrist any time suspicion arises. Sometimes the symptoms mentioned above do not turn out to be indicative of affective illness, and sometimes minimal symptoms turn out to be clues to substantial disease.

Signs of Depression and Mania

An outline of the common signs associated with depression is presented below, followed by an outline of the common signs associated with mania.

DEPRESSION

1. *Signs of Low Mood*

    a. **Withdrawal:** A person suffering from depression may lose interest in activities that once gave him or her pleasure and may participate less in social interactions.

    b. **Negativism:** A person who is usually tolerant of many different viewpoints may become excessively skeptical when depressed. He or she may stubbornly resist the suggestions, orders, or instructions of others.

    c. **Unhappiness:** A depressed person may experience persistent sadness or frequent crying.

2. *Signs of Lowered Self-Attitude*

    a. **Self-deprecating, guilty, or self-blaming comments:** When depressed, a person may put himself or herself down with comments such as "I'm such a failure; I wonder how you stay with me." A depressed person may also accept blame for problems that do not exist or are clearly not his or her fault.

b. *Expressions of hopelessness:* In depression, a person may experience unusually persistent pessimism and may express despair in suicidal statements or acts.

3. *Signs of Decreased Vital Sense*

a. *Decreased attentiveness to oneself or to one's tasks:* A depressed person may neglect his or her appearance and let assignments at school, housework at home, or projects at work slide.

b. *Decreased energy:* A person with depression may complain of fatigue and lack of energy or "motivation." He or she may have particular difficulty getting activities started, especially in the early morning hours.

c. *Decreased ability to concentrate:* Depression often makes it difficult for a person to think through a problem and, thus, to initiate and complete a complex mental task. A usually avid reader may begin to read many books but may not finish them. A faithful correspondent may be unable to write.

d. *Excessive indecisiveness:* A depressed person may vacillate between choices to an unusual degree and may defer decision making to others. This may be true even for simple decisions that were previously made routinely.

4. *Additional Signs*

a. *Change in weight or in eating patterns:* Decreased appetite leading to weight loss is a common symptom of depression. However, in some depressives (especially those whose depressions come during a particular season of the year), appetite and weight increase.

b. *Change in sleep patterns:* Characteristically, a depressed person's sleep is interrupted, especially in the early morning hours (2 to 6 a.m.), but in some depressives sleep is excessive and waking is difficult.

c. *Change in sexual interest and activity:* Characteristically, sexual interest and performance are decreased in a depressed person.

Very close observers may be able to recognize other changes in a friend or family member as depression takes hold. The depressed person's mood often slips. He or she may function unusually poorly in the morning and improve somewhat as the day goes on. The person may also experience *anxiety attacks*; these periods of apprehension or fear can include physical signs such as shortness of breath, sweating, or shaking.

In contrast, many of the signs associated with mania are the opposite of those described for depression, as the outline below shows.

MANIA

1. *Signs of Elevated or High Mood*

    a. *Excessive cheerfulness:* A manic person may be unusually elated.

    b. *Irritability:* A person with mania may become irritable even over small matters, especially when one attempts to "reason" with him or her.

    c. *Anger beyond irritability:* When suffering from mania, a person may develop a haughty or superior stance that is not usual for him or her.

2. *Signs of Increased Self-Attitude*

    a. *Expressions and acts of unusual optimism:* These can show poor judgment. Unfortunately, the overconfident, manic person's energy is often channeled into inappropriate, dangerous, or indiscreet behavior. A normally conservative person may undertake foolish or risky business ventures, may engage in sexual indiscretions, or may speak in overly critical or judgmental terms, often at inappropriate times and about sensitive subjects.

3. *Signs of Increased Vital Sense*

   a. *Increased energy:* A person with mania may appear tireless in the face of physical and mental efforts that would greatly tax an unaffected person. He or she may feel completely refreshed after just a few minutes or hours of sleep.

   b. *Increased activity:* The increased energy of mania often translates to a host of new projects at work, a seemingly insatiable desire to socialize, or greatly increased participation in sexual activities.

   c. *Excessive talking:* A person with mania may seem to talk endlessly, sometimes jumping haphazardly from idea to idea. Alternatively, a manic person may adopt an unusually abrupt and short or clipped manner of speaking to others.

4. *Additional Signs*

   a. *Change in eating patterns:* A manic person may have a voracious appetite or may be too busy to eat.

   b. *Change in sleep patterns:* When suffering from mania, a person feels less need for sleep, so sleep is usually decreased.

   c. *Change in sexual interest:* Sexual interest is often increased in a manic person.

The DSM-III

One of the tools psychiatrists use to recognize depression and manic-depressive illness is the *Diagnostic and Statistical Manual of Mental Disorders* (DSM-III), published in 1980 (and revised in 1987) by the American Psychiatric Association. To be diagnosed with a particular disorder, a person must have a certain number of the signs and symptoms listed as features of that disorder in the DSM-III. By this system, individuals can be assigned to a diagnostic group. For example, Mr. Smith might be diagnosed with disease X because he shows at least two of the characteristics of X on one list and six of those on another but does not show any of the symptoms of disease Y on a third.

The approach of the DSM-III has, to some extent, standardized the diagnosis of psychiatric conditions. With it, pychiatrists in different areas of the country have been able to overcome local trends that might favor giving one diagnosis rather than another to a patient with a given set of signs and symptoms. The DSM-III influence, in fact, extends around the world, lending a standard vocabulary to the international dialogue between psychiatrists and making their exchange of knowledge more efficient and more fruitful.

Not only psychiatrists benefit from the DSM-III. The manual also makes it easier for other physicians and other health professionals to accurately diagnose mania and depression in their patients. Those who fit the manual's description of depression or manic-depressive illness (see Figures 1 and 2) are more likely to be helped by accepted forms of treatment than are those who cannot be easily categorized.

The limitation of the DSM-III, or any checklist of symptoms, is that it does a better job of deciding who should be called depressed (or manic) than it does of describing the ill person's experience. Too much emphasis, for example, is placed on the patient's sadness and not enough on the potentially devastating effects of the feeling of hopelessness.

Perhaps most important, deciding that a patient meets the

A. At least five of the following symptoms have been present during the same two-week period and represent a change from previous functioning:

1. Depressed mood
2. Markedly diminished interest or pleasure in almost all activities
3. Significant weight loss or weight gain
4. Increased sleep or inability to sleep
5. Slowed movements or inability to sit still
6. Fatigue or loss of energy
7. Feelings of worthlessness or excessive guilt
8. Diminished ability to think or concentrate
9. Recurrent thoughts of death or suicide

B. Not due to brain injury, sadness following a loss, or another mental illness

Figure 1. Symptoms of a major depressive episode. (Adapted from American Psychiatric Association, 1987.)

A. A period of abnormally and persistently elevated, expansive, or irritable mood

B. At least three of the following symptoms:

1. Inflated self-esteem or grandiosity
2. Decreased need for sleep
3. More talkative than usual
4. Flight of ideas or subjective experience that thoughts are racing
5. Wandering attention
6. Increased activity
7. Excessive involvement in activities that have a high potential for painful consequences

C. Symptoms sufficiently severe to cause marked problems with one's job, social activities, or relationships

D. Not due to brain injury or another mental illness

Figure 2. Symptoms of a manic episode. (Adapted from American Psychiatric Association, 1987.)

DSM-III criteria for depression or manic-depressive illness tells us nothing about the causes of the disorder. This is understandable, since our knowledge of causes is still emerging. Although the DSM-III is a state-of-the-art guide, in the long run we will want to substantiate the clinical diagnoses outlined in the DSM-III with the anatomical and physiological abnormalities that we believe underlie the symptoms.

CHAPTER

The Causes of Depression

In sooth I know not why I am so sad;
It wearies me; you say it wearies you.
But how I caught it, found it, or came by it,
What stuff 'tis made of, whereof it is born,
I am to learn.
　　　　—William Shakespeare,
　　　　　The Merchant of Venice (1600)

Today's psychiatry has been lucky to find medications and other therapies that help patients. Yet, although the available treatments usually relieve depression and manic-depressive illness, we don't know exactly how they work. This would be easier to live with if we were satisfied with the current methods of treating affective disorders, but we recognize that more can be done. Learning about the causes of depression can make treatment less mysterious and more powerful.

Pharmacological Causes

A valuable clue to the origins of depression was provided by patients being treated for high blood pressure with a drug called reserpine. Doctors noticed that some of these patients seemed to

23

get depressed. When it was shown that reserpine caused deple-
tion of a group of neurotransmitters called *catecholamines*, psychiatrists reasoned that deficiencies in this kind of chemical
messenger in the brain might lead to depression. The basic theory
was supported by research that showed that two kinds of medication for depression, the tricyclic antidepressants and the monoamine oxidase inhibitors (see Chapter 19), increased the availability
of a cathecholamine called *norepinephrine.*

Too little norepinephrine, depression. Too much norepinephrine, mania. Too good to be true. Other neurotransmitters, some
belonging to the more general family called *biogenic amines*, were
soon implicated. And since several of the tricyclic antidepressants
were shown to increase the levels of a neurotransmitter called
serotonin, researchers thought that there might be at least two
kinds of depression, one characterized by low norepinephrine and
another by low serotonin. So close, and yet so far. Other neurotransmitters, including dopamine and acetylcholine, and their
receptors have become suspects in the chemical mystery of
depression.

The story doesn't end with depression, however. A number
of drugs—such as steroids and phencyclidine hydrochloride (PCP,
or "angel dust")—have been found to cause symptoms of mania
as well.

The intrigue, in fact, extends beyond these pharmacological
or drug-related, culprits. Depression and manic-depressive illness
are frequently seen in the setting of many other bodily (physical)
disturbances, making physicians wonder that the link might be.

Neuronal Causes

The first group of bodily disturbances consists of the *neuronal
abnormalities*, that is, those involving injury to, or malfunction
of, the brain. *Huntington's* disease is an example. People with
this disease, a rare genetic condition which usually becomes apparent only in adult life, experience a steady decline in their
intellectual abilities. They also become unable to control their

movements. Of particular interest to scientists studying affective disorders is the fact that symptoms of manic-depressive illness often appear early in the course of Huntington's disease. Understanding more about the earliest stages of this disease, then, may teach us more about mania and depression.

The same is true for *Parkinson's disease*, another more common neuronal abnormality, in which movement disorders result from the death of nerves connecting two regions within the brain. These nerves use the neurotransmitter dopamine to communicate with one another. People with Parkinson's disease often suffer from depression, and psychiatrists treat their mood disturbances in the same ways they treat major depression in patients without Parkinson's disease. Interestingly enough, when the abnormal movements in patients with Parkinson's are treated with the drug L-dopa (a protein in the body from which dopamine is made) patients sometimes develop symptoms of mania.

Yet another neuronal cause of depression is *stroke*, the sudden interruption of the blood supply to part of the brain. Studies show that of the patients who suffer strokes, about 25 percent go on to develop clinical depressions. Johns Hopkins psychiatrist Dr. Bob Robinson and colleagues have found that such injuries to the brain might cause depression by destroying nerves that use the catecholamine transmitters we spoke of earlier. What's more, they have observed that the location of the injury within the brain predicts how likely it is that depression will occur and how severe it will be when it does occur (see Figure 3).

Endocrinologic Causes

The second group of bodily changes linked with affective disorders consists of the *endocrine abnormalities*. The endocrine system is the body's network of glands. Glands release hormones into the bloodstream that affect every organ in the body.

The thyroid gland, located in the neck, is a major part of the endocrine system. When too little thyroid hormone is released into the blood, a condition known as *hypothyroidism* results. Hy-

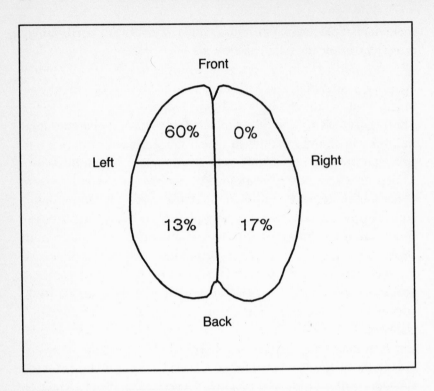

Figure 3. A cross section of the brain, showing the percentage of patients who experience a major depression after suffering a stroke that affects one of the four brain regions. (Adapted from R. G. Robinson et al., 1984, with permission.)

pothyroidism can cause muscle aching, hair loss, constipation, and diminished hearing. It also commonly causes a form of depression.

Cushing's disease, also an endocrine abnormality, results from excessive stimulation of the adrenal glands by another gland called the pituitary. This overstimulation causes the adrenals to produce too much of the hormone cortisol. People suffering from Cushing's disease often have round, moonlike faces and rotund abdomens and suffer from diabetes and high blood pressure. Some develop symptoms of mania or depression. All these symptoms can also occur in people taking steroids, which are actually cortisol-like drugs, for other medical conditions.

Genetic Causes

Although we have covered much territory with the pharmacological, neuronal, and endocrinologic causes of manic-depressive illness, we have yet to review perhaps the most significant cause of all—*genetic abnormalities*. In Chapter 10 we discuss the evidence suggesting that a predisposition to suicide might be influenced by genetics. This is almost certainly related to the genetic abnormalities thought to predispose individuals to mania and depression.

The facts are convincing. Studies in identical twins, whose genes are exactly the same, show that if one twin suffers from depression or manic-depressive illness, there is a 50 to 90 percent chance that the other twin will develop the illness at some time. For fraternal twins, who share only half their genetic material, the presence of depression or mania in one twin is associated with a much smaller (10 to 25 percent) chance of depression or mania in the second twin. You may be wondering why the identical twin of an individual with major depression or manic-depressive illness would have only a 50 to 90 percent, rather than a 100 percent, chance of developing the illness. After all, both twins have exactly the same genes. The answer is not complete yet. One explanation may be that the disorder in the affected twin is the result of a nongenetic cause, as we discussed above. A second explanation may be that only a vulnerability to affective disorders is passed through the genes and that environmental factors may trigger a genetically loaded gun in the affected twin. Such environmental factors could include difficult relationships, financial trouble, legal problems, and the medications and bodily disorders mentioned above. All of these possibilities continue to be proper subjects for research. As discussed in Chapter 8, alcoholism may be an important environmental contributor to, as well as a consequence of, depression.

Adoption studies also lend weight to the view that manic-depressive illness is inherited. Children of affectively ill parents who are adopted into families having no history of these conditions still show three times as many depressive disorders as the natural children in the family.

Genetic research holds great promise for the millions of Americans who must face affective illness. Within the next decade, psychiatrists and molecular-genetics scientists using new methods that center on the workings of DNA should be able to discover which types of depression and manic-depressive illness are inherited and which are not. With currently available methods and cooperative families, research studies can be expected to tell us even more about where on our twenty-three pairs of chromosomes the causative genes are located. Already, regions of chromosomes 6, 11, and X have been linked to manic-depressive illness in several families (see Chapter 12). In these families, nearly all family members affected with the illness carried the unique chromosomal marker. Nearly all unaffected family members did not.

In the long run, we will see that "genetics versus environment" is often a misleading debate. *Phenylketonuria* (PKU), a condition that causes mental retardation, is a good example. Scientists discovered that PKU is caused by a genetic error in the way that phenylalanine, an essential amino acid found in food, is metabolized. The phenylalanine accumulates and gets processed into toxic substances that cause brain injury. While the cause of the illness is genetic, the treatment is environmental. All infants are now tested for PKU, and the parents of those found to have the condition are instructed to feed their infants foods that do not contain phenylalanine. Retardation is avoided, or at least minimized, in this way.

Genetics versus environment in depression and manic-depressive illness? Not likely. Far from making the environment irrelevant, new understandings that come from genetic research will probably lead to a fresh look at environmental factors in the prevention and treatment of mania and depression.

PART TWO

THE EXPERIENCE
OF DEPRESSION

*If this life be not a real fight, in which something is eternally
gained for the universe by success, it is no better than a
game of private theatricals from which one may withdraw
at will. But it feels like a real fight.*

—William James,
The Will to Believe (1897)

CHAPTER

The Patient's Experience

I am now the most miserable man living. If what I feel
were equally distributed to the whole human family,
there would not be one cheerful face on earth.
      —Abraham Lincoln (1809–1865),
         in a letter to his wife, Mary Todd Lincoln

Psychiatry's efforts to conquer depression and manic-depressive illness have as their guiding force the motivation to improve the lives of those who suffer from these illnesses. Listening to the experiences of our patients, often as inspiring as they are tragic, has imbued our efforts with personal significance. Whether you suffer from severe mood disturbances yourself, have witnessed a family member or friend struggle with such disorders, or have developed an interest in these illnesses for other reasons, the personal accounts that follow will enrich your perspective on depression and manic-depressive illness. With permission of those involved, we have edited these accounts in order to preserve anonymity.

Nicole

My life changed dramatically at 21. It was 1947 and I was a newlywed living in Alexandria, Egypt, and was very excited about starting a family. My husband was handsome and intelligent. I loved him completely. But I began to think that I shouldn't have gone through with the marriage. I couldn't enjoy anything anymore. I had married the man every woman in town had wanted to marry, yet I was unhappy with him. I began to sleep less, getting up at four or five in the morning. I didn't speak.

My friends tell me that when I am depressed my face changes. In French we call it *"le masque."* I feel as if all the muscles in my face are tense, and I can't smile.

During this first depression, and during each of the depression that followed, I focused on the difficulties of life. I brooded over the things I should have done to become a success. I felt guilty about not having tried harder. Life seemed to be cheating me out of pleasure, and though I didn't consider committing suicide, I began to hope that an accident or a murderer would end my suffering. I had a vague idea that the secret police were eavesdropping on me.

I never saw a psychiatrist, but I improved gradually. After about a month, I could feel the depression lifting, feel myself returning to a normal life.

My husband and I had our first child, a beautiful little girl. I was very happy. We were living with my husband's father and were often joined for dinner by my two brothers-in-law, but I didn't mind. I understood that it would be many years before we could afford more.

In 1950, however, I began to brood over our cramped quarters and lack of privacy. My husband tried again and again to explain our financial situation, but despite the fact that we clearly could not afford the change, I insisted on a home of our own. I had no interest in caring for my daughter; warning that I would not return until another apartment was rented, I went with my aunt to her home in Cairo.

I lay in bed for hours each night unable to fall asleep. When I did finally drift into sleep, nightmares plagued me. I imagined myself on a dark street being stalked by someone, and I was running, always running. My appetite was gone, and I refused to eat. I wanted deeply to be dead, but still would not act on my desire.

My aunt brought me to a small hospital run by nuns, and a psychiatrist there gave me some medication. It didn't seem to help. After a few days I insisted on moving back to my aunt's house.

I received at this time, months after leaving Alexandria, a picture of my daughter. It was winter, and she was standing in the park in open sandals. I decided to return home to take care of her, but I was very nasty to my husband and his relatives. Looking back, I think my depressed mood had swung toward mania.

I immediately insisted on control of the family finances. I would talk constantly, walk endlessly around the house, and never get tired. I hardly needed to sleep. I bought many expensive things we neither needed nor could afford. I told my husband that his brothers would be allowed to dine with us once a week at most.

Gradually, I improved, but not before a year of my life had been spent on this seesaw.

For the next five years I remained healthy. I returned to teaching mathematics, my career before my marriage. I enjoyed my students immensely. Since both my husband and I were working and making money, we hired a woman named Maria to help take care of the house. She became a close friend, and I shared with her my most intimate thoughts.

Maria took ill with cancer of the esophagus during 1956 and died in hospital. Without realizing it, I became depressed again. I was convinced her death was my fault because I had failed to take proper care of her. Mixed with my profound guilt was an equally powerful sense of panic. What would happen to me without her? How would I manage the house?

Work became hell. I could not concentrate long enough to solve even a simple math problem. I gave unsatisfactory answers to my students' questions, often stopping in the middle of writing an equation on the board, unable to go on. I needed a great deal of encouragement from my husband just to go to school each morning.

At this time a doctor advised ECT [electroconvulsive therapy; see Chapter 20], but my mother objected, and I never received the treatment. I wish that I had been treated, as I continued in this terrible state for nearly two years.

It was not until 1968 that my fourth depression took hold. My daughter was now a lovely young woman and was attending a university in Egypt. She was involved with a handsome boy with little character. We wanted very much for her to leave him and Egypt, where the quality of life was bad, and live in the United States. After much convincing, she finally went to America.

She was very unhappy living outside Egypt. She missed her young man terribly. My husband missed his daughter equally. Our attempts to join her in America met with no success. The Egyptian government refused to give my husband, who had earned two Ph.D.s in mathematics from the Sorbonne in France, permission to leave the country.

To make matters worse, a few months later my husband suffered a heart attack. I blamed myself. I thought that if I had allowed my daughter to stay and marry her boyfriend, my husband would not have been so upset and would not have been stricken. Fortunately, he recovered. I did not.

Finally, we received, as a favor from a highly placed government official, permission to emigrate. We left everything we owned in Egypt—the work of 40 years—and brought with us only $300 in cash.

In the United States I continued to be depressed. I hated my apartment and could not find a job. My thoughts of suicide were stronger than ever, and I seriously considered throwing myself out a window. Each time, however, I stopped short when I thought of how my daughter would feel. Because my husband knew I was thinking of suicide, he brought me with him each day to the university where he taught mathematics.

When my depression lifted, it switched again into mania. I broke my apartment lease, not caring about the troubles this could bring. I purchased many things which were too expensive or not needed. I felt as if I had to be doing something every minute of the day.

Finally, two years after the depression had taken hold, and three months after the mania began, I returned to myself. I found a job teaching Spanish and French, and I began working as a translator part-time.

By 1981, I was experiencing what I hope was my last depression. I sat in the corner at work and said nothing. My husband began to translate my assignments at home during the evenings to appease my employer. I saw two psychiatrists who counseled me with no success.

Finally, my daughter's husband arranged for my admission to Johns Hopkins. I reluctantly capitulated (but only after he threatened to leave the family) and received five ECT treatments. These helped me greatly, and I rapidly improved. I now take tricyclic antidepressants [see Chapter 19] and see my doctor occasionally for a checkup. I have not relapsed, and I feel really well.

I am very proud of four things in my life. First, in spite of my illness, I have raised a wonderful daughter who is a source of joy to my husband and me. Second, I am happy to have come through all this with my marriage intact. My husband and I have remained young at heart and joke about many things. Third, I am proud to have had the courage to come to the United States and to become an American citizen. Last, I feel good about having mastered five languages and having worked as a translator.

My advice to those who suffer from depression or those who must witness the suffering of a friend or family member is this: Never lose hope. You are not alone, and as bad as things are, suicide is not the answer. I can remember times when I was convinced I would never be able to enjoy life. I write today as a woman with a husband of forty years, a loving daughter, and a firm conviction that the joy in my life has outweighed every sorrow.

Joann

I am 38 years old, divorced, and have no children. I have a serious psychiatric illness which is currently under control. During the course of my illness, I have lost my family, friends and home. My life has been disrupted. My career is on hold. I have had enough pain and loss to last a lifetime. Still, I count myself a very lucky person. I'm alive. Many people who have had my illness are not—they took their own lives. I give thanks every day for being alive and for the many blessings I have. I see happy years stretching out in front of me.

I spent this morning working in my garden. Although it is only mid-February, my daffodils are already poking their heads up, and the roses are showing new bright-red shoots. I felt so much joy as I found each new wonder, and I marveled that my flowers are waking from another winter.

As I settle down now with my dog, my coffee, and my books, the contrast between today and this time three years ago is so stark as to seem unreal. Yet that terrible time was every bit as real as my joy today, and it still feels so close that I can reach out and touch it.

Three years ago I wasn't planning a garden. I was thinking about where I could buy a gun to kill myself with. I was in agony, caught up in an excruciating, unrelenting mental anguish that worsened with each day. I could see no end to the blackness that engulfed me, and I knew I could not endure much longer.

What had happened to me over the few brief months since I put my first tulip bulbs in the ground? What had happened to turn my life upside down and bring me to the verge of ending it? Not knowing then about my illness, I searched in vain for a reason for my suffering. Nothing, it seemed, had happened to make me feel so terrible. Yet, in a few short months, every drop of color had been slowly drained from my life—so gradually that I didn't notice it happening. Then, all of a sudden, there was no joy left in my day. There was no pleasure in getting up to a new morning, in being with friends, or in doing any of the million and one things I love to do. All that stretched in front of me was an aching loneliness and emptiness. Nothing had meaning. Nothing brought pleasure. I wanted desperately to laugh and have fun again. But the pain grew worse. There was no respite from the feeling of impending doom. I lost all hope that things would get better.

For a while, work took my mind off my troubles and I could escape briefly, but this source of relief was short-lived. Work first became a trial of endurance and then a major source of anxiety. I had to struggle every morning to force myself out of bed. I cried as I literally walked around in circles trying to decide what to wear. At work, I kept a mask on, pretending that nothing was wrong. I stayed in my office as much as possible, at first to avoid people so that they wouldn't notice how red and swollen my eyes were from crying. It was terribly important to me to conceal my pain from everyone, especially since I could not explain it. I struggled to keep control of my emotions. I didn't understand what was happening to me, and I felt as though no one else would either. Withdrawal seemed to be the answer. Soon, though, the problem became so severe that I became unable to maintain the illusion that everything was okay. I became increasingly and noticeably forgetful, in-efficient, and irritable. Mail, phone messages, and requests began piling up. I was so confused that I couldn't seem to clear anything away. I couldn't concentrate enough to read. Even minor chores began to seem very difficult.

Dealing with other people is usually one of my strong points, but I was getting into real trouble there, too. I often misinterpreted the words and actions of others and blew small incidents all out of proportion. I recall yelling at a co-worker right in the hallway one day and dissolving into tears in my boss's office the next day. I was horrified at my own behavior and couldn't understand why I was getting so upset in the first place. I felt so awful and guilty. I began thinking of myself as a terrible worker who had managed to fool people for a long time but who was about to be exposed as a stupid, careless employee who couldn't do her job. Work became like walking a tightrope; I felt as if I would fall off at any moment and get fired. Though I was making very real mistakes, my perception of reality was not accurate. It never occurred to me that were I really that bad, someone would have talked with me about my performance long ago.

By this time, my days were one long, confused haze, and I was choking with fear and anxiety. By the time I would get home from work, I would be exhausted. I stopped cooking, cleaning, and even walking the dog. I lost weight. Sleep became my only escape, and I tried to sleep as much as I could. I never woke up really refreshed. At my worst, I would snap awake in the very early hours of the morning, with a terrible knot gripping my stomach. I was always tired, with neither the energy nor the desire to do anything. I experienced headaches, muscle aches, stomachaches, and nausea. I felt physically and emotionally awful.

All throughout, few of my friends and no one in my family knew how sick I was. I tend to be a private person normally, and it is very easy to lose track of people and time in the winter. I stopped answering the phone most of the time, and I didn't call people. They just thought I was busy or not at home. On the rare occasions when I did see people socially, I was subdued. How could I ever explain to them what was going on when I didn't understand it myself? After all, I was always kicking myself for feeling so bad without a reason, always telling myself to just snap out of it. I couldn't risk someone else lecturing me as well. I was embarrassed by my weakness, what I saw as my self-indulgent moaning, and I didn't think other people would be able to handle being around me. At the very time when I needed other people the most, I isolated myself from them.

Every aspect of my life had been disrupted. No one ever said anything to me about getting help. No one ever suggested that I might be sick. No one was aware of the signs of my illness, nor was I. It's pretty scary in retrospect to think how sick I was and to realize that no one knew.

This story might well have ended very differently than it did. I was alone, in terrible pain, and with an overwhelming sense of hopelessness about the future. I had consulted doctors for years about a wide array of physical complaints that they could find no explanation for. I had worked very hard in therapy for several years after my divorce and had made substantial changes. Indeed, I happened to be in therapy during this entire, terrible time. I felt that I had done everything I could do to fix myself but that I was in worse shape than I had ever been. Suicide seemed to be the only answer, and I knew that I would have to plan carefully if I were to be successful.

But I am a truly lucky person. At a time when my life was bleakest, my therapist finally convinced me to see another doctor. It was a very hard thing for me to do. Although the therapist told me that I might have a biochemical depression, I had never heard of any such illness. I thought that if such an illness really did exist, it would have to be pretty rare. I didn't believe that I could be lucky enough to have a real illness, with a name, characterized by the symptoms I had been experiencing. That, in itself, would have been vindication enough, without any consideration of treatment possibilities.

A measure of my pain was the fact that, for two weeks, I would not allow the therapist to set up an appointment. While that might seem odd, I believed this doctor to literally be my last hope. If he said that I didn't have the illness called depression, there would be no other way out but to commit suicide. Finally, I consented to the appointment.

After talking with me carefully in order to take an extensive personal and family history, the psychiatrist put the picture together. He explained that there is, unfortunately, no litmus test for my illness. Accurate diagnosis, essential for effective treatment, depends on the care, skill, and experience of the diagnostician.

The psychiatrist prescribed a tricyclic antidepressant [see Chapter 19]. Within a month I began feeling better, and all I needed to keep hanging on was the hope that this gave me. By summer, despite the fact that I had had a very serious car accident in the interim, I was almost back to my old self. There was a joint decision for me to stop psychotherapy in June. I no longer needed it for support, and the medication was relieving the symptoms of my depression. Since then, I have been maintained on a tricyclic. I see a local psychiatrist to monitor my medication and help me keep track of my moods.

Since being placed on medication, I have on a few occasions experienced very mild and brief symptoms of depression, but they have gone away quickly and not incapacitated me. I believe these have been tempered by the medication. I know now that depression is a recurrent illness that can be controlled, but one for which there is currently no cure.

Looking back, everything seems so obvious to me now. I ask myself how it is that I didn't know what was happening to me, nor did my friends, family, co-workers, or health consultants. I am an intelligent, highly educated, aware individual. Why didn't I recognize my symptoms and know that I had an illness called depression? Why didn't I see a connection between this episode and similar, if not so serious, ones I had had in the past? The plain truth is that I was woefully and nearly fatally ignorant of some basic facts about depression. I didn't know that it is an illness, in exactly the same way that we think of cancer or diabetes, for example. I couldn't list the warning signs or recognize a constellation of symptoms. I didn't know the treatment modalities. I didn't know that depression is an illness characterized by recurrences. Although we are an extremely health-conscious society these days, mental illness still has a stigma associated with it that makes it mysterious to us, even though basic, important facts are known and effective treatment is available.

Peter

April 4, 1983, was a gorgeous spring day. The banners were waving in a balmy breeze, and short sleeves were the order of the day. I was excited and excitable, hopeful and expectant—certainly, a man at ease in his surroundings. In this setting my experience with manic-depressive illness began.

It was the opening-day game for the Baltimore Orioles, a team I have followed religiously for years. Better yet, "The Birds," as true fans call them, were ahead. Normally, I would have been overjoyed by a win in the home opener. But in the sixth inning, in the midst of celebrating with friends and my favorite sports team, I began to feel fuzzy, blurry-eyed, unsure of myself, afraid of the crowd, uneasy about the height of our seats over the field. I became very quiet.

My friends noticed the change in my mood on the way home: my short answers, the lack of life in my voice, my pregame excitement extinguished. I recall telling them that I felt that my mind was tired, but now I know that on that day I came face-to-face with my first biochemical depression.

I was born and live today in a small town in West Virginia where I practice medicine. I am fortunate to have a loving, caring wife who is also my best friend. We have three children, ages 12, 6, and 4. The 6-year-old is a boy, surrounded by his sisters in age.

Looking at my family tree, I should not have been surprised to have psychiatric illness at some point in my life. My great-grandfather exhibited times of great activity and great melancholy, according to my grandmother's writings. She herself was diagnosed with manic-depressive illness, but she was never treated. My father was an alcoholic who died as a result of his drinking. His life included great business successes and failures, several divorces, and frequent depressions.

With what I suppose was an inherited predisposition, I met with several stresses during the months before the Orioles' opening day. My grandmother, with whom I enjoyed a very close relationship all my life, passed away. In the same month, my father died. My wife and I were expecting a new baby at the end of April. My workweeks at my office climbed to seventy-five hours.

The low and fearful mood I experienced at the game was just the beginning. For weeks, I progressively lost more and more motivation, curiosity, and creativity. My appetite waned, and my sleep was disturbed. At first, I sought relief in my office and tried, literally, to work through it. I realized that this was not a solution when one morning I could not force myself to get out of bed and go to work.

I saw a doctor and got medication, but it seemed to work too well, and I became manic. I became oblivious to reason and experienced extreme financial difficulties as a result of spending sprees. Delusions of grandeur, sexual indiscretions, and extreme irritability threatened my marriage.

For five months, I experienced cycles of mania and depression every ten days. My doctor tried changing the dosage of my medication. My wife, Karen, and I both knew what was sure to follow with each new cycle, and the feeling was oppressive. We were unable to count on anything enjoyable in the future, knowing that I would be unreachably high, severely depressed and anxious, or in transition from one to the other.

When I look back on that period of several months, I wonder at the fact that my wife stayed with me. I am thankful that she was able to remember things about me when I was well that helped to carry her through this low point of our time together.

Still seeing no improvement, I became a research volunteer at the National Institute of Mental Health (NIMH) on September 14, 1983. As time passed, a more effective medication for my particular brand of bipolar disorder was found; the proper dosage was determined, and I improved immediately. While it was extremely difficult being away from my family and my work during my stay at the NIMH, I had many introspective moments to think about piecing my life back together.

Before I returned home, I began to carefully rebuild my marriage, faith, friendships, and business. My wife never wavered, nor, at its foundation, did my faith. Former friends looked askance, as if they could not believe that I was now "normal" after being on a "psych ward." Present friends were happy for my health and interested in the new genetic principles behind the biochemistry of my illness. I called each of my own patients to inform them of my renewed well-being and to assess their intentions. This was an incredibly difficult experience, but it was central to my plans to reestablish myself professionally.

Today I continue to take only lithium carbonate [see Chapter 19]. Minor mood swings still come and go with this medication, but not of a severity near that which I experienced during 1983. I have not missed a day of work or of active living since March 26, 1984, when I first returned to the practice of dentistry. I complain at times about the increased appetite, some weight gain, and the occasional fatigue that I experience with the medication, but I continue to take it. Staying well is so important to me.

I went trout fishing recently—one of the few things I love more than the Orioles. When I returned home, Karen told me, as she often does, how happy she was to have me healthy. I was happy to hear that and to feel that. The baby I mentioned as an added stress in 1983 is a beautiful little girl named Erica Marcia. She was 5 years old on May 1, 1988.

I reflect often on the five years since her birth and am thankful we are all together. I don't know whether we need to be concerned about Erica or our other children having this illness. I hope and pray always that the researchers working on affective disorders have continued success. In the meantime, we all need to help educate Erica and others and give them hope for the future. There is a great deal more to be done in the world.

The Family Experience

The mind is its own place, and in itself.
Can make a heav'n of Hell, a hell of Heav'n.
—John Milton,
Paradise Lost (1674)

Affective illnesses seldom affect just one life. The ripples of pain touch family members and friends who become, in some ways, co-victims. The essay that follows, written by a woman whose husband took his own life, has served to remind us that the suffering of millions of depressed Americans reflects the pain of tens of millions of others. We share it with you not to criticize the doctors involved but to further Elizabeth's desire to support those families in which even well-intentioned and well-designed treatments have failed.

Elizabeth

It is truly remarkable how much one's life can change in unexpected ways. I still find it hard to believe that Daniel is no longer alive, that a person with whom I shared fourteen years of marriage has simply ceased to exist.

My husband's illness began when he was a young adult. He suffered three bouts of severe depression, all after we had married and begun to have children. The last episode ended in suicide.

To appreciate fully the impact of depression on Daniel, it is necessary to have a sense of what he was like when well. There was, first of all, always a dry wit that complemented his unusual good looks. Although he had attained great success in real estate, he maintained a humility that allowed him to communicate as readily with maintenance workers as with his business associates. He was a wonderful, involved, and loving father to his two children. He was a spontaneous, romantic, steadfast husband.

The demands of Daniel's career did not prevent him from volunteering extensively to help the handicapped, participating in church activities, and playing golf, tennis, and squash. Fishing was one of his favorite pastimes.

Each of the three times my husband became ill, his entire personality changed. He completely lost interest in the things that normally brought him pleasure—especially being with people. He would feel extremely anxious and unable to concentrate. He had several other symptoms, such as early morning awakening, extreme fatigue, decreased appetite, and rapid weight loss. When he felt these symptoms building, he was terrified that he would take his own life and said that he felt as if his actions were not under his control.

I found it difficult to fully appreciate what the psychiatrists told me. My husband had a mental illness. I was frustrated. I had been raised in a family in which we were taught to kick ourselves in the rear and get on with life when we got down. I had no knowledge of the disease process of depression, and I, therefore, had no understanding of Daniel's situation. When he said that he felt like killing himself, I said, "Don't be ridiculous!"

The first time Daniel required hospitalization was in 1962. He had slit his wrists after weeks of extreme anxiety and depression. After cutting himself, he had called his psychiatrist and driven himself to the hospital. He told me later that he remembered looking at his hands and saying, "What the hell have I done?"

When I received the news, I actually fainted. Mental illness, my husband. From that day on, I lived in fear for his life.

Daniel had, at age 5, lost his father to alcoholism and been raised by his mother. Because of this dramatically sad childhood, the doctors tended to look at his illness exclusively as the result of a "bad life story."

Although my reaction was one of shock at Daniel's first hospitalization, it was one of relief during the two that followed in 1969 and 1975. I felt relieved that Daniel was the responsibility of the doctors rather than me. Since that first attempt on his life, whenever my husband began to feel depressed, I was terrified. I remember that the social worker at the hospital told me not to show that I was anxious because Daniel might feed off that emotion and spiral further down. I found it very difficult, however, not to mirror his feelings in some ways.

We were incredibly attached to each other. While there had been terrible times during the fourteen years Dan and I were married, there had also been tremendously exciting times. He was impulsive, energetic, and risk-oriented. He had achieved great financial success that had given us the freedom to enjoy a wide range of experiences. I have often wondered whether I would trade the long-lasting periods of excitement and relatively short-lived low times for the average of both. I know that I wouldn't.

During the second episode, Daniel was hospitalized for six months. I simply tried to keep my head above water—working as a teacher, taking care of the children (then 1 and 6 years of age), and going to the hospital daily. I had never been under such stress.

My family was supportive throughout Daniel's illness, but his family hid from the problem. His mother never visited the hospital, and I worried that some of his immediate family members actually blamed me for his illness. I never felt any guilt personally, however. Dan told me and some of his friends that I had kept him alive many times when he would otherwise have wanted to die.

Friends were, for the most part, there for us. Of course, some people shied away and treated Daniel as if he had leprosy. The fact that someone in their social and financial circle had fallen victim to depression made them too aware that they themselves could be vulnerable to mental illness. "If it could happen to him," they thought, "it could happen to me." But his good friends finally accepted Daniel's depression as a real illness, like diabetes, for example, and visited him regularly when he was hospitalized.

The final episode of depression was the most difficult for my children. They were 7 and 12 years old. Dan and I sat down and explained depression as a mood illness that had to be treated in the hospital with medicine. They were completely confused; they still saw their father as loving and responsive. The only change they noticed was the irritability that came before the severe depression. My 7-year-old became quite anxious—afraid at bedtime and fearful of my leaving her. My older daughter coped better.

Daniel felt responsible for his depressions. Some of his psychiatrists had rejected the possibility of a biochemical basis for his depression. One made an unfortunate comment that seemed to set a limit on how much loss of self-control still permitted hope for recovery. "Once [one depression] is all right, twice is shaky, but three strikes and you're out," he said. This comment haunted Daniel, and he repeated it to several of his friends.

In 1975, Daniel's doctors did begin treating him with a variety of medications. These were, however, difficult for him to tolerate physically. When they failed to work satisfactorily, he was started on ECT which, after three treatments, seemed to be making him better. After the third treatment, however, Daniel shot and killed himself while alone on a visit at home.

Daniel's doctors and I have since discussed the tragedy and the troubling aspects of his treatment. They not only carried out a review of his care but, in 1976, conducted a training program for the staff of the small hospital on the care of the depressed patient at risk for suicide.

I grew up in such an idyllic way; I never knew life could be so tortured. I had never contemplated personal disaster, and to this day I wonder at the strange and painful detour my life has taken at a relatively young age. At one time in my life, there was nothing that could make me anxious. I was never scared of anything. Now I realize Chicken Little was right—the sky can fall in. Maybe I don't like knowing all there is to know about life.

My daughters know more than I knew at their ages. They are still coming to terms with their father's death. We talk openly about him—a good thing, since most memories are of laughter rather than sadness. They continue to learn and to grow. Counseling has helped.

My life and the lives of my children have been changed. But we go on. My career is a new and exciting one. My children are a constant source of personal pride. My marriage, when Daniel was healthy, was a string of chapters from a storybook romance. I cherish that.

CHAPTER

The Physician's Experience

It was, of course, a grand and impressive thing to do,
to mistrust the obvious, and to pin one's faith in things
which could not be seen.

—Galen (A.D. 129–199),
On the Natural Faculties

Almost ninety years ago Emil Kraepelin best described manic and depressive conditions (in several hundred patients) as two parts of a "single disease process." He also reported, however, that he had found nothing wrong in the brains of affectively ill patients who had died and that he could offer no truly effective treatments. Many psychiatrists were, therefore, skeptical about his claim that these conditions were bodily diseases. Turning to psychoanalytic methods, they generated a new optimism about the prospect of relieving the suffering of mentally ill patients. The pessimism of some in the traditional psychiatric community, they said, had led to a false belief that chronic hospitalization for most patients with serious mental illness was inevitable.

It would not be long, however, before psychiatrists using psychoanalysis realized that it did not work in most severely depressed or manic patients. Some psychiatrists took notice of these and other disappointing results and, for many years, did not treat the most seriously ill individuals.

In the past fifty years, we have witnessed the evolution of new medical treatments that are helpful and generally safe in the treatment of the seriously mentally ill. Many of these, including tricyclic antidepressants and lithium, are described in Chapter 19. The development of these agents helped to encourage the view that major forms of mental illness can be distinguished from each other as distinct disease entities, illnesses that yield to relatively specific medical treatments.

While writing this book, we have been reminded that although many things about psychiatry have changed, others have not. We have discovered that each of us, though we attended medical school decades apart, had classmates and instructors who wondered if psychiatrists were "really doctors." Some seemed to think of psychiatry as separate and apart from the rest of medicine. Each of us has come independently to the conclusion that much of the power of psychiatry rests not in its isolation from medicine but in its marriage to the time-honored medical processes. Diagnosis, prognosis, and treatment should be applied to persons with manic-depressive disorder just as they are to diabetics.

The Public Health Experience

One of the domains of public health is *epidemiology*, a discipline that studies the distribution of illness in the community. The strategies of psychiatric epidemiologists at various times have shaped psychiatrists' views of their patients and their roles as physicians.

Through the 1960s, a fair number of the psychiatrists working in epidemiology viewed all human suffering as being of one sort. They tended to lump together a variety of psychiatric disorders as simple variations on the general theme of human suffering. The famous Midtown Manhattan Study (1962), for example, concluded that 80 percent of midtown Manhattan residents had some psychiatric symptoms. Some psychiatrists looked to stress as the source of this general malaise. Once the world could be made a less stressful place, they theorized, the all-too-common forms of psychic distress could be minimized. This view of the world was undoubtedly well intentioned, and probably helpful to those experiencing stress from life events, but it did little to direct psychiatry's clinical or research efforts.

By the close of the 1970s, psychiatrists responded with explicit criteria defining specific disorders (e.g., the DSM-III criteria discussed in Chapter 2). They then began documenting how widespread those disorders were within the community. The Epidemiological Catchment Area (ECA) survey, beginning in 1980 and involving 18,000 people in five cities, developed from this process. Its goal was to document the rates of specific mental disorders, rather than to explain the human condition.

The study demonstrated that affective disorders are among the most common psychiatric illnesses facing Americans. In Baltimore, 4 percent of the population was found to have affective disorders. Of these people, 1½ percent were suffering from depression, ½ percent from mania, and 2 percent from a less severe mood disturbance known as dysthymia. Many more people had experienced one of these conditions at some point in their lives prior to the time of the study. Other widespread health problems in the community included phobias and alcohol or drug abuse.

What's more, the study found that people with recent, documented mental disorders were not being adequately treated. In Baltimore, only 15 percent of such individuals had visited a professional for psychiatric symptoms in the previous six months, and only 8 percent of their visits were to professionals specializing in mental disorders. Results from other cities were similar.

The refinement of its epidemiological tools has given psychiatry another powerful weapon against affective disorders. Stressing specific illnesses and insisting on accuracy in diagnosis promises that psychiatry's public efforts will be better focused.

CHAPTER

The Plot Thickens

My life felt so cluttered and obstructed that I could hardly breathe. I inhabited a closed, concentrated world, airless and without exits. I doubt if any of this was noticeable socially: I was simply more tense, more nervous than usual, and I drank more. But underneath I was going a bit mad.

—A. Alvarez,
The Savage God: A Study of Suicide (1971)

The Atypical Depression

We have said that some persons classified as dysthymic have true clinical depressions while others are better understood as chronically unhappy. Many of those who fall into the clinically depressed group have what is called *atypical depression*. This moderately severe form of depression is characterized by a course that is both chronic and intermittent—long periods of illness punctuated by sudden, brief intervals of relief. When the relief is really hypomania, the condition is called *bipolar II disorder*.

Atypical depression seems even more closely associated with distressing life events than is typical depression. Long-term follow-up of atypically depressed patients, however, supports the idea that they too suffer from an illness, not just a reaction to circumstances.

People with atypical depressions are less likely to be impaired in their work, activities, or relationships than are those with typical (and more severe) depressions. They often oversleep (especially on weekends), overeat, and suffer from symptoms of anxiety. Their symptoms tend to be linked to what we call *periodic disorders*, such as premenstrual syndrome or *seasonal affective disorders*. Finally, they are vulnerable to developing abnormal behaviors like eating disorders, alcoholism, drug addiction, or pathological gambling.

Anxiety States

Severe forms of anxiety—phobias, panic attacks, obsessions, and compulsions—may occur alone or as part of a depression. Although the dramatic anxiety symptoms may obscure the depressive symptoms, recent research has shown that severe anxiety symptoms often respond to traditional antidepressant medications. Family studies suggest that anxiety states are related to genetic forms of clinical depression.

A *phobia*, such as claustrophobia (fear of confining spaces), is an unreasonable fear that is closely related to one particular situation. The phobia is often recognized as ungrounded by the person suffering with it, but it is frequently still sufficiently severe to cause him or her to avoid particular places or activities. When the situation is impossible to avoid, extreme feelings of anxiety can develop. Social phobias, such as fear of being in crowds or of being alone, are the ones most commonly associated with depression.

The anxiety state associated with depression need not, however, be provoked by a specific situation. In *panic attacks*, the individual experiences sudden and overwhelming feeling of fear that is accompanied by shortness of breath, hot or cold flashes, heart palpitations, chest discomfort, or even muscle cramps. The symptoms can occur while the person is watching television or driving; they are not wedded to one set of circumstances.

Finally, atypical depression can keep company with obsessive-compulsive symptoms. These take three forms:

1. A recurrent thought (*obsession*) which is unwanted and recognized as inaccurate, embarrassing, or trivial but which recurs despite attempts to banish it. For example, one might be unable to shake the idea that one has been exposed to dangerous germs.

2. A recurrent and irresistible activity (*compulsion*) that is designed to banish an obsessive thought. For example, someone with an obsession about contamination with germs might feel compelled to wash his or her hands repeatedly.

3. A compulsion which seems unrelated (but may in fact be related) to obsessive thoughts and which is characterized by the repetition of simple behaviors until they "feel" correctly done. For example, one might feel compelled to turn a light switch from on to off repeatedly until it "feels" completely off.

Abnormal Behaviors

ALCOHOLISM AND DRUG ABUSE

Substance abuse often complicates the lives and treatment of people with affective disorders. Persons with atypical depression sometimes learn that they can alter their moods by using alcohol and other drugs. They self-medicate.

Some patients say they drink alcohol because it "gives [them] instant energy." Others say they do it to "calm" their nerves or to "anesthetize" their emotions from the pain of depressive illness. The relief is only short term, however, and the longer-term problem of addiction may be even more serious than the depression itself. The same is true for self-medication with other drugs, in-

cluding anything from prescribed pain relievers to illicit intra-
venous street drugs.

Once addiction sets in, the pain of withdrawal, or even the
fear of withdrawal, can be perceived by the individual as more
distressing than the underlying depression. He or she may not
be motivated, therefore, to stop. Usually little improvement can
occur in mood or addictive behavior, however, until the person
is withdrawn from alcohol and/or other drugs for a substantial
period of time (usually two to four weeks).

After withdrawal, many patients will experience considerable
relief of depressive symptoms without further treatment. If standard treatments are needed, they will be more effective at this
time. In addition, the postwithdrawal period allows the psychiatrist to explore whether a mood disorder is present at all. Intense
substance addiction and its withdrawal can produce apathy, low
mood, and other depressive symptoms even in people without
affective illness.

EATING DISORDERS

Anorexia nervosa is a disordered behavior centered on pur-
suing thinness. An anorexic's attempts to suppress appetite and
avoid calories can lead to malnutrition and even death.

Depression can cause some people to become anorexic. On
the other hand, anorexia can produce its own fatigue, inability to
concentrate, and moodiness. It may be difficult to determine
whether these symptoms are coming from an underlying depression or from the eating disorder and subsequent state of starvation.
For this reason, confident diagnosis sometimes cannot be made
until the state of starvation is reversed.

Bulimia is an abnormal behavior related to anorexia. Many
bulimics, in fact, have been anorexic, and some people suffer from
both simultaneously. The abnormal goal in bulimia is to eat (sometimes to binge eat without limit) but to remain thin. Many bulimics

who first suffered from anorexia report that they simply want to maintain their very low weight but feel irresistible urges to eat immense quantities of food. They control their weight by starving themselves between binges or by ridding themselves of calories by making themselves vomit (called "purging"), taking laxatives or diuretics (water pills), or overexercising.

Many bulimic patients also have the atypical form of depression and, in our experience, some have brief periods of mild hypomania. They would therefore fit the description of bipolar II illness.

Bulimics often report that overeating will soothe their nerves or boost their moods when they feel anxious, bored, or depressed. Many consider purging to be a way of maintaining low weight and "fixing" what they see as abnormal eating. The purging, however, also makes them feel they have done something wrong or abnormal. It may make them feel even more depressed.

The vomiting, laxative abuse, and diuretic abuse accompanying bulimia can cause severe metabolic abnormalities. Singer-songwriter Karen Carpenter apparently died from the effects of low potassium caused by bulimia. Still, most bulimics are not in a state of starvation when they come for treatment, and compared with anorexic patients, their underlying mood is more easily assessed. When depression is found to play a role and is treated, bulimics often feel less urge to binge and purge.

PATHOLOGICAL GAMBLING

Another behavior to which some depressed people become addicted is gambling. In this behavior, technically referred to as *pathological gambling*, the craving is for excitement rather than winnings. The addicted gambler, therefore, tends to gamble until the money runs out. He or, less often, she may borrow or steal money to support the gambling habit. This is one more example of how individuals with atypical depression adopt behaviors designed to improve their moods.

Some behaviors can be quite bizarre, such as inflicting minor cuts or burns on oneself to release anxiety. All of them can also occur in many people who do not have affective disorders. Even among those with clinical depression, abnormal behaviors can become so strong that they represent bigger problems than the underlying depression. What's more, they can persist even when the depression is treated and relieved.

Periodic Disorders

PREMENSTRUAL SYNDROME

Premenstrual syndrome (PMS) in its simplest form includes irritability, bloating, abdominal pain, and occasional depressive symptoms. In some women, however, a full-blown depressive illness—low mood, feelings of worthlessness, a sense of hope-lessness, decreased energy, and impaired concentration—waxes and wanes with the menstrual cycle. This PMS/depression (PMS/D) can itself take one of three forms:

PMS/D Type 1: Since untreated depression usually lasts several months, depression among women of childbearing age
often endures through many menstrual cycles. Symptoms
of depression in these patients will usually worsen in the
premenstrual period. This worsening may be due to particular hormonal changes during the menstrual cycle, or it may
simply be due to having both PMS and depression at
once—a sorry coincidence. The exact cause is still unknown.
PMS/D Type 1 is probably the most common menstrual
cycle–mood interaction in depressed patients.
PMS/D Type 2: This less common form of PMS/depression is
sometimes an illusion. Several studies of both depressed
women and men show that some will have depressions that
inexplicably recur every twenty-eight to thirty-five days.

When this occurs in a menstruating woman, there will often be successive menstrual cycles during which, by pure coincidence, depression is getting started just as the premenstrual week begins. If one charts moods and menstrual cycles over longer periods of time, however, it is easy to see that the depressive peaks and menstrual periods not only come together but also eventually move apart.

PMS/D Type 3: Finally, there are a few individuals whose cyclic mood disorder becomes wedded to the menstrual cycle. These women usually have a rather abrupt onset of symptoms of depression or mania or of a mixed state (sometimes accompanied by delusions and hallucinations) just prior to each menstrual period. The symptoms can be quite disabling during the premenstrual time period but can disappear suddenly once menses starts. A similar marriage between hormonal changes and depression can occur during puberty, pregnancy, childbirth, termination of pregnancy, thyroid disease, and hormonal (e.g., estrogen) therapy. The reasons for this are still unclear, but it is the subject of much research.

SEASONAL AFFECTIVE DISORDERS

The occurrence of depression each winter and/or brief, mild hypomania each spring is called _seasonal affective disorder_. The pattern was first recognized by the psychiatrist Jean Esquirol in the 1800s. It was not until a decade ago, however, that psychiatrists at the National Institute of Mental Health related the pattern to differences in exposure to sunlight. They were impressed by the history of a man who had carefully charted his depressed and hypomanic moods for fourteen years, revealing a regular pattern of mood changes. One December, his depression was shifted to hypomania when researchers exposed him to bright artificial light, mimicking springtime.

Artificial bright light was later widely tested and proved to be effective in relieving winter depression (see Chapter 20). Its effectiveness was originally ascribed to the fact that artificial light, just like sunlight, inhibited the production of a hormone called *melatonin*, produced by the pineal gland in the brain. The theory came under question, however, when it became clear that melatonin was suppressed equally in patients who improved with bright light therapy and in those who did not.

More research is necessary to explore the relationship of seasons and light not only to depression but also to the other mood disorders. The connection has already yielded the surprise bonus of bright-light therapy—a new and apparently very safe treatment.

CHAPTER

Healthy People Suffer Too

The sound of her silk skirt has stopped.
On the marble pavement dust grows.
Her empty room is cold and still.
Fallen leaves are piled against the doors.
  Longing for that lovely lady
How can I bring my aching heart to rest?
  —Han Wu-Ti
    (Chinese poet, 157–87 B.C.)

Understanding the Response
  to a Loss

Society has its own expectations of what constitutes a "normal" response to personal tragedy. People close to a dispirited individual seem to have an internal barometer of whether the reaction of their friend or family member matches the depth of his or her loss. Either through similar experiences of our own, or through hearing of the experiences of others, we develop an empathic sense of how people typically respond to a variety of sad events. We expect different reactions from a person who has survived a spouse or a child than we do from a person who has been fired from a job, has moved away from a friend, or has lost a pet. We place the tears, loneliness, anxiety, fear, and anger on a spectrum and have strong opinions about what amount of sadness seems "right" or "healthy." This comparison to the norm leads to thoughts, or even comments, such as "You'd think Bill would have pulled himself together by now" or, conversely, "Three weeks, and Marilyn's already dancing on his grave."

Episodes of affective disorder often occur after losses or stressful events, but these episodes can also overtake a person's life in good times. The well-known "grief response" that comes with the death of a loved one, on the other hand, would not exist without the special sad event. While grief has predictable common elements from individual to individual (including sadness, disturbed sleep, frequent sighing, feelings of isolation or anger), speeding its resolution depends on understanding how the person interprets his or her loss: What it means.

The fact that the grief response which follows a death and the sadness which can, for example, follow a divorce are not illnesses does not imply that they fall any less under the umbrella of the psychiatrist than do affective disorders. Psychiatry's central concern is the alleviation of a person's suffering, whether that suffering is the result of disease or demoralization. Most people, however, will not need professional help at all following losses.

The depth and unique expression of the normal response to a loss is sculpted from the peculiarities of the particular relationship that has been lost. The strength of the bond between a husband and his wife, a woman and her job, or a student and his or her career plans is the energy that powers the emotional response when the bond has been broken. Knowing the extent of the distress and how to lessen it can be achieved only when the psychiatrist knows what the person believes has been lost. Depending on the husband and his feelings, the death of his wife can be equivalent to the death of his lover, his only friend in the world, his business partner, his caretaker, or even his tormentor. It can represent the end of youth, the end of fertility, the end of love, or the rebirth of the same. These relationship issues place sadness and suffering in the realm of the life story (see Chapter 15).

While some characteristics of demoralization are common, the events that trigger suffering can be quite individual. *Demoralization* is a state of weakened spirit, courage, or staying power; it is the experience of being thrown into confusion. The person who loses a highly prized job may be saddened when he or she sees former co-workers, walks past corporate headquarters, or rummages through old business letters. The mother of a handicapped baby may become despondent when she sees normal children playing together. Similarly, the length of time before sadness resolves will be highly individual. For some, a new pet can wholly replace one that has died. For others, no pet ever could, and the very sight of the same kind of dog, for example, will always provoke real despair. It is important that the meaning of an individual's loss be legitimized by those around him or her. People do not generally contrive grief, and lessening their suffering depends upon accepting and understanding their subjective sense of how their lives have been changed.

Personality traits (see Chapter 13) of the demoralized person influence his or her emotional response to the particular loss. Any trait (e.g., extroversion) will be an asset in facing some stressful situations and a vulnerability in facing others. These traits will even determine, to an extent, which events are perceived as losses to begin with.

A 36-year-old man with diabetes and depressed mood was being seen in psychotherapy by a young psychiatrist many years ago. He did not have many of the characteristic symptoms of the clinical syndrome of depression and related his feelings of low mood to his progressive physical disability. He had always been an independent, self-reliant man. He grew up deprived of material, though not of spiritual, resources. His wife said he had not only been a devoted and good provider for the family but had encouraged and supported her in further education so that she could financially sustain the family in his absence. She was grateful and devoted to him. His encouragement made her feel more self-confident and worthwhile.

Both the man's wife and his psychiatrist were surprised at the depth of the patient's depressed mood. They become particularly alarmed when he began to discuss the "logic" of suicide. He explained that he had become sexually impotent (a complication of severe diabetes). As a proud and devoted man, he reasoned that he was depriving his wife of a complete marital partner and that the "right" thing would be to end his life decisively despite the "understandable" and "sympathetic" objections of those close to him.

The psychiatrist considered whether he should change his diagnosis to depression and refocus treatment toward medications. Clearly, there was nothing he could do about the patient's diabetes and its effects on sexual potency. After consultation with a senior colleague, however, he refocused not on disease, nor on stress, but on the patient's independence. He conducted a session with the patient and his wife during which he asked her why she opposed the planned suicide. "He loved, supported, and provided for me, and now I want to do the same for him," she said.

"Are you able to allow yourself to be taken care of?" the psychiatrist asked the husband. "Can you accept that your wife places less of a priority on sexual fulfillment than on the other gratifications of sharing her life with you?"

With this focus on his personality trait, the patient, who was more honest and devoted than he was proud of his independence, made a substantial reassessment of his and his wife's situation. After several emotional discussions with his wife over the course of a week, he became much brighter in mood and dropped all thoughts of suicide. Although he was still very ill from diabetes, he did not feel his life would deprive his wife of fulfillment. This, in turn, gave his life more meaning.

This case illustrates the powerful role of personality traits (here, independence) in determining a person's response to a loss. It also shows that recognition of the traits as both strengths and vulnerabilities can help patients.

Chronic Illness as a Loss

Even when independence is not the most prominent trait in a person's personality, the loss of his or her confident lifestyle to a chronic illness like diabetes or epilepsy can bring real sadness.

The idea that our bodies are losing ground to a disease or are declining with age not only reminds us of our mortality but can divert or cast doubt on our life plans. Almost 50 percent of patients with serious illnesses suffer initially with low mood and demoralization. Most, but not all, of them come to some accommodation with their condition.

The ill person's most adaptive response might be to try to incorporate the requirements of illness into his or her lifestyle. If dialysis treatments will be needed on an ongoing basis, for example, it would be beneficial to try to view oneself, the dialysis technician, and the physician as a team working to protect the essence of one's life. There will be some machines and routines that take getting used to. Individuals who are sensitive to surrendering control of their bodies should participate in their care by striving to learn about their illnesses and to make positive lifestyle changes to improve their chances for good health.

When a chronic illness is felt to be terminal, many individuals are able to focus not on time lost but on how to best use the time remaining. Still, many will suffer low mood and may need help getting back to equilibrium.

Likewise, new perspectives on life can be born in the wake of events like a heart attack. It is normal and proper to reexamine one's values, immediate goals, and long-term aspirations when the brevity of life has been trumpeted by a threat to one's health. Before adjustment is secure, some people will experience a response not wholly different from the grief response.

The Grief Response

In "Mourning and Melancholia," Sigmund Freud compared the grief response to major depressive disorder, or melancholia:

> The distinguishing mental features of melancholia are a profoundly painful dejection, abrogation of interest in the outside world, loss of the capacity to love, inhibition of all activity, and a lowering of the self-regarding feelings to a degree that finds

utterance in self-reproaches and self-revilings, and culminates
in a delusional expectation of punishment. This picture becomes
a little more intelligible when we consider that, with one ex-
ception, the same traits are met with in grief. The fall in self-
esteem is absent in grief; but otherwise the features are the same.

The response of survivors to the loss of a loved one—the *grief
response*—was best described by Erich Lindemann, a psychiatrist
who, in 1941, interviewed the bereaved relatives of people killed
in the Coconut Grove fire in Boston. Other people have described
a similar reaction to the loss of a body part as the result of injury
or illness. While the intensity, duration, and texture of the grief
response depends on the meaning of the loss to the individual,
Lindemann was able to define recognizable stages of grieving.
Those who have suffered the recent loss of a loved one may find
their experiences described in the paragraphs that follow. Painful
as they are, the numerous feelings and reactions are normal components of grief. With time, they resolve, leaving cherished memories behind.

    ⌞. The first stage of grief, which may be short-lived, can be
described as a period of numbness—a fog. A patient of ours who
lost her husband, for example, described the days following his
death as a hazy time during which, like an actress playing a widow,
she went through the motions of making funeral arrangements,
greeting mourners at her home, and contacting the family lawyer.
She was surprised that she was able to attend to details, even
alerting those at work to the projects that needed immediate
attention. Others describe overriding feelings of bewilderment
that make planning difficult.

    This sense of detachment, numbness, or "shock" may be na-
ture's way of protecting us from the full force of significant losses.
The dulling of our feelings (and our conviction that we must take
care of others) serves as a first line of defense against what might
otherwise be an onslaught of sadness, fear, or anger.

    As the cloudiness of grief recedes, an intense yearning for the
lost person takes its place. Depending on the loss and what it
means to the individual, this phase of grief can last months or

even years. There is often preoccupation with images of the deceased. Some people even describe momentarily feeling their loved one's presence or hearing or seeing their deceased husband or wife or son or daughter. This is especially common when they are falling asleep or awakening.

Intense sadness, loneliness, and, frequently, anger are characteristic of this second stage. The full significance of how life has changed seems to settle in. There are often feelings of isolation or abandonment. Frequent tearfulness can be expected, along with deep sighing and sleep disturbance. Concentration can be impaired, and one's interest in the outside world may diminish. Some people describe feeling exhausted, but many feel restless, with no direction for their energy.

The possessions of the lost child, the mementos of the lost lover, photographs of the lost spouse—all can evoke intense emotions, as if the energy of the relationship is being translated to inanimate substitutes. This attachment can also extend to social symbols of the deceased person, such as a cemetery headstone. The object can be highly individual—a game-winning ball, for instance, representing the life of an athlete in the family who has passed away.

Grieving people report dreams about the deceased that frequently include, for example, a living representation of the loved one who has passed away. Likewise, when the grief response follows the loss of a body part, the body might be depicted intact in dreams. Typically, there is a sense of disappointment on awakening to reality.

Daydreaming may also erase a loss temporarily. The despair reinstates itself, however, when the daydreamer "comes back to the real world" and realizes that he or she had been thinking that the loss never occurred.

The third stage of grief involves a restless, aimless, and disorganized effort to restructure one's life. It is as if strategies to fill the void created by a loss are being tried against the continued backdrop of an overriding sense of despair. This searching phase blends with the final stage of grief—real reorganization. Intense sadness and loneliness have receded to some extent, and life's problems (money, dating, children, school), rather than the particular loss, take center stage.

Even while the sadness recedes, certain places or dates or even figures of speech will bring the loss back to mind. At such times, people report a welling up of grief that can be accompanied by "butterflies" in the stomach, tightness in the throat, and tearfulness. The number of experiences that can bring on a wave of grief will diminish with time, and with each episode the sadness gradually lessens. Still, depending on the individual and his or her sense of loss, some events or people or locations may provoke a revisitation of grief for many years, perhaps for a lifetime.

The final stage of grief (which may take several years to resolve) also frequently sets the stage for a genuine peace with the memory of the loved one who has passed away. New understandings of life's challenges and blessings can be achieved, leaving memories, to be sure, but ones that can bring a feeling of warmth or happiness, as well as the occasional tears.

Although the grief response can be thought of as having phases, they are not as regular or as distinct as night and day. Not everyone experiences each phase. Furthermore, the experience of the response varies due to the difference in who was lost (child, spouse, parent), how he or she was lost (illness, homicide, or suicide), and what cultural influences exist in the community in which the grieving person lives (religious, ethnic, and geographic).

Complicated Grief Responses

One of the painful aspects of the response to a loss (whether it be a death or a disappointment) can be judging one's own physical and emotional reaction as unjustified or as a sign of weakness. In fact, many different types of emotions are actually normal parts of working through a loss. No one is immune to sadness. Sometimes special circumstances complicate the responses to a loss to the point that professional help may be needed. Most of these complicated responses are unrelated to clinical depressive disorders.

Despite Freud's observation that self-esteem does not fall during normal mourning, guilt is not an uncommon feeling, particularly after the death of a loved one with whom the surviving person had an ambivalent relationship. In some cases, the surviving person may feel freed, not just from the burden of caring for an ill person, but also from a dominating or even fear-inspiring relationship. Alternatively, there can be a great sense of unfairness about the death of someone the survivor had come to rely on in life. Some people may experience unusually intense anger when the death was very sudden or when, in the grieving period, secrets about the deceased are revealed which are injurious to the survivor.

One of our patients, Gene, the father of a young man who had just died from cancer, told us that he had lost his temper when his son's doctor attempted to console him in the hospital. "You had three months to get him well and you blew it!" Gene yelled. "Three months!"

Gene hadn't realized how close to death his son had been. His life had changed dramatically with his son's fatal illness. Hadn't they planned to tour college campuses in just a few weeks? Wasn't there another season of high school football around the corner? Hadn't they talked about handing down the family business? For Gene, being confronted with a lack of control over his future was a maddening experience. An illness, something he could not have predicted or avoided, had taken his child. He was enraged at his limitations as a human being, at his impotence against an invisible, but collosal, enemy.

He also felt singled out. Why was this happening to his family? What kind of fairness could exist in a world where an innocent person could die at such a young age? Everything Gene had been taught about goodness returning in kind seemed to be violated by the loss of his son.

Getting past his anger was easier for Gene after he recognized it, and acknowledged it, in a consultation session. Further discussions of feelings with close friends and family members helped him focus more realistically on his own loss and on the needs of his other family members. Gene's problem was not major depression, but the emotional response was strong and potentially injurious.

Grief responses that are complicated by being delayed, hidden, or prolonged may also be a source of concern to the bereaved person and those around him or her.

One special type of bereavement, the loss of a loved one through suicide, is almost always followed by a somewhat complicated grief response. In working with bereaved families after the suicide of a family member, we have found that nearly all such families need help with their reactions.

Three complications after suicide can hinder the normal grieving process:

1. Some family members may become emotionally estranged from other members because of the tragedy.

2. Many close family members tend to blame themselves or the victim unrealistically.

3. Some family members or whole families may spend an enormous amount of energy trying to persuade themselves and others that the death was not a suicide.

Although we came to know some families only after the suicide of a loved one (see Elizabeth's story, Chapter 6), we have been gratified to see how directly the issue can sometimes be handled. On the other hand, even among families we had worked with prior to the suicide, some felt unreasonable guilt despite the fact that they had made every effort possible to intercede.

One example of an unrealistic perspective was that of a husband whose wife had fatally overdosed on aspirin. The entire family had been involved in her care following several hospitalizations. Family members stayed with her constantly, brought her for frequent outpatient visits, and personally administered her prescribed medicines. They had removed all medicines, except the aspirin, from her reach—they were unaware that aspirin could be lethal.

After the suicide, the husband recognized that neither he nor the other family members understood the dangers of an aspirin overdose. However, he blamed himself for not being a good husband, and he believed that he had not been close enough to his wife. He felt strongly about this even though he had quit his job to nurse her at home and had accompanied her to each of her doctor's appointments for the previous two years. He also tried to persuade himself that his wife's death was not a suicide (although a suicide note was left) but an accidental overdose.

In counseling the husband, we actively challenged his feelings that he had not been attentive and affectionate to his wife. We recalled forty occasions when he had escorted his wife to the hospital. On hearing this recounted, he was better able to accept that he had, in fact, been a devoted spouse. As he overcame his guilt, he also came to acknowledge that the suicide had been an intentional, but irrational, act arising from his wife's depressive mind-set.

Despite the fact that most suicides are the fatal outcome of depressive diseases, there is a strong tendency among the bereaved to feel somehow responsible for contributing to the lost person's sadness, for failing to alleviate it, or for missing signs of it. Moreover, a husband, for example, may feel guilt because he sees himself as not having been a powerful enough reason for the deceased to have wanted to stay alive. It is crucial, therefore, that the bereaved person take the time to evaluate the relationship accurately, often by describing its elements to a friend, family doctor, or psychiatrist. Most often, it will be seen that far from pushing the victim toward death, a survivor had been his or her anchor in life.

Beyond guilt, there can be an overwhelming sense of abandonment, with or without anger. An element of choice on the part of the victim is frequently felt to be present when someone dies by suicide. A bereaved wife, for example, might wonder,

"How could he do this to me? How could he leave me alone with the kids?" In fact, the overwhelming sadness and hopelessness that are symptoms of depression, together with possible false, but terrifying, fears, have taken control away from someone who goes on to suicide. Suicide is usually not an act of informed and free choice. It is almost always the result of pain and of false pictures of the world seen through the dark lenses of very severe major depression.

When a suicide is not preceded by repeated bouts of mental illness, there can be sudden concern among survivors that the suicide was a personal expression of anger or antipathy by the deceased. Family members of these suicide victims may search for another reason behind the suicide and may be relieved to find one—even a disease. They may become alarmed at the prospect that the disorder, being genetic, could "kill" other family members. In fact, genetically predisposed family members sometimes will experience a clinical depression after such a loss.

We counsel such survivors about the treatability of the disorder and the relative rarity of suicide as long as prompt medical attention is sought when symptoms appear. While it would not be unreasonable to keep an eye out for trouble, there is no need for temporary and normal emotional responses of family members to alarm other members.

The Role of Psychiatric Evaluation

While major depression can occur without any precipitating loss, it is important to know that a distressing event can indeed bring about an episode of the disease. Therefore, simply being able to identify the likely source of one's distress does not mean that demoralization or the grief response alone explains the full extent of the problem. When the symptoms of depression are present, they must be taken seriously, and a psychiatrist should be contacted.

One of our patients, an 8-year-old girl named Crissy, was

admitted to the child psychiatry clinic for declining school performance and repeated statements of suicidal wishes. These had started within a month after the patient had witnessed the violent murder of her mother by her father, which occurred about a year before her evaluation.

The first impression was that Crissy's reaction was "justified" grief, not major depression. After all, she had watched a terribly traumatic scene. The fact that her grandparents, with whom she lived, were unable to speak about the event or answer her questions about it was taken to explain why her reaction was so prolonged. The youngster, we thought, was unable to get her worries and concerns addressed and, therefore, remained grief-stricken.

With family counseling Crissy slowly improved, but after nine months she again lost interest in school and expressed suicidal ideas. This time, antidepressant medication was tried, and it proved extremely effective within three weeks. What became clear through a review of the course of the illness and its rapid response to treatment was that the loss Crissy had experienced had triggered her first depressive episode.

The intensity of a loss is fully known only to the person who experiences it. There is no litmus test for evaluating which events are worthy of deep sadness. To one person, losing a job might simply bring transient anger over the fact that his or her full potential went unnoticed. To another person, being fired might be taken as a devastating confirmation of preexisting fears that he or she is simply unlikable.

Similarly, a loss is not always something physically here today and gone tomorrow. Losses can evolve, as is the case when a person's plans for his or her life (whether they be for money or for a happy marriage) ultimately fail to materialize. In such cases, real sadness can result from the loss of what might have been. Self-images are painfully revised. Questions about the meaning of life suddenly dominate one's thoughts.

Anyone who has experienced a significant loss and feels unable, despite sharing feelings with friends or family members, to put that loss in perspective and become constructively involved again in life should consider getting a psychiatric evaluation. Certainly, a person who feels overwhelmed by sadness beyond the normal grief response we have described should be seen by a physician. Even if the person's response turns out to be normal, knowing that nothing is awry will help the individual.

The Big Picture

One of the by-products of a significant loss is that it can bring us to new understandings of life. People who suffer heart attacks, for example, may revise their vocational goals and enjoy their families more. Time seems short.

Author Robert Pirsig offered his own understanding of death, arrived at in part through the loss of his son, Chris:

> The loops eventually stopped at the realization that before it could be asked "Where did he go?" it must be asked "What is the 'he' that is gone?" There is an old cultural habit of thinking of people as primarily something material, as flesh and blood. As long as this idea held, there was no solution. The oxides of Chris's flesh and blood did, of course, go up the stack at the crematorium. But they weren't Chris.
>
> What had to be seen was that the Chris I missed so so much was not an object but a pattern, and that although the pattern included the flesh and blood of Chris, that was not all there was to it. The pattern was larger than Chris and myself, and related us in ways that neither of us understood completely and neither of us was in complete control of.
>
> Now Chris's body, which was part of that larger pattern, was gone. But the larger pattern remained.

CHAPTER

Depression and Suicide

My mother died seven years ago by her own hand. My father found her when he returned home from work that Friday, her body already cold. . . .

She was 55 when she died. She looked behind her and saw a wasteland, never willing to accept that she was loved by many and had richly contributed to the lives of friends, family and strangers. She perished because she allowed herself to be deceived by her own mind into believing she was worthless. . . .

She taught me the most valuable lesson of my life: no matter how bad the pain is, it's never so bad that suicide is the only answer. It's never so bad that the only escape is a false one. Suicide doesn't end pain. It only lays it on the broken shoulders of the survivors.

—Anne-Grace Scheinin,
"My Turn," *Newsweek*,
(February 7, 1983)

The Statistics

Suicide is the tenth leading cause of death in the United States; 12 out of every 100,000 Americans take their own lives each year. The rate among those aged 15 to 24 has doubled over the past twenty-five years (see Figure 4), making suicide the second leading cause of death in young people.

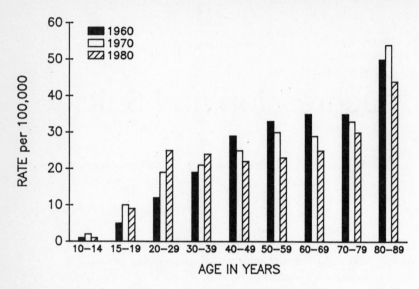

Figure 4. Suicide rate by age group per year. (Adapted from a study by Dr. David Neubauer done in Dade County, Florida.)

The Risk Factors

DEPRESSION

As many as 15 percent of severely depressed people take their own lives. As with any abnormal behavior, it is difficult to predict who will commit suicide. Psychiatry has, however, identified important risk factors. The most significant is depression; 50 to 95 percent of suicides (depending on the community studied) are due to this illness.

A study conducted in Sweden described further the connection between affective disorders and suicide. For at least fifteen years, researchers observed and psychiatrically evaluated 1823 male inhabitants of an area they called "Lunby." Among those who carried no psychiatric diagnosis, the suicide rate was 8 out of every 100,000 people each year. For the segment of the population diagnosed with psychiatric conditions other than affective disorders, the suicide rate was much higher—83 per 100,000 people each year. Most striking, for those diagnosed with affective disorders, the rate was 650 per 100,000 people each year!

The study also demonstrated that the depth of a man's depression relates to the likelihood that he will commit suicide (see Table 1). No suicides occurred among those diagnosed as suffering from a mild form of depression. Those men with moderate depression had a suicide rate of 220 per 100,000 people each year. Severely depressed men, however, showed the startling suicide rate of 3900 per 100,000 people each year (nearly 4 percent). The study results reveal what scientists call a "dose-response" curve: the higher the dose of mood disorder, the more likely the response of suicide.

Biochemical studies also support the relationship of major depression to suicide. Those who take their own lives seem to have different levels of the substance 5-HIAA in the fluid surrounding the brain and the spinal cord. This substance is formed when serotonin, one of the brain's chemical messengers, or neurotransmitters, is metabolized. In one study, 5-HIAA levels appeared to predict which of the depressed subjects would commit suicide within a given period of time. Behaviors are complex, however, so much more investigation will be required to explain these findings.

One of the most dangerous periods for suicide in a severely depressed and suicidal person occurs when his or her condition begins to improve or when he or she is discharged from the hospital. At this point the depressed person may have just enough

Table 1. Depression Severity and the Suicide Rate among Men in "Lunby"

Depression Severity	Suicides per 100,000 Persons Each Year
Mild	0
Moderate	220
Severe	3900

Source: O. Hagnell et al., 1981.

energy to carry out a plan for suicide and may not yet have enough optimism to reject the idea. It is a widely held misconception that people who talk about plans for suicide never carry out those plans. They sometimes do.

Preventing suicide in a severely depressed patient is, of course, a psychiatrist's final chance to prevent a loss due to depression. Research into the causes of major depression and manic-depressive illness offers hope for victories earlier in the process.

OTHER FACTORS

A number of specific groups have been found to be at higher risk for suicide than are other segments of the population. Men are three to four times more likely to take their own lives than are women (although women *attempt* suicide three to four times more frequently). The elderly have a suicide rate three times higher than the general population (see Figure 4). Those living alone, those who have attempted suicide in the past, and those who refuse to be evaluated by a psychiatrist also seem to be at increased risk. Overall, white individuals (in the United States) commit suicide more often than do blacks.

Alcohol- and/or drug-dependent people are yet another high-risk group. A recent study suggests that the dramatic increase in the suicide rate among people under 30 years of age may be related to an increase in drug abuse.

And what if other family members have committed suicide? Would a person whose mother and brother took their own lives be at increased risk to do the same? Could a tendency toward suicide be programmed in a person's genes? A study of the Amish community in Pennsylvania lends some support to this possibility.

Old Order Amish is a very religious society whose members live, work, and marry among each other according to strict rules. Amish life offers a number of protections against suicide. There is little alcohol or drug abuse, virtually no unemployment, and a strong social support system and an extended family network to ward off loneliness. The act of taking one's own life, forbidden by religious law, is referred to by the Amish as "the abominable sin." Only twenty-six suicides occurred from 1880 to 1980. While many families during these hundred years included members who suffered from affective disorders, fifteen of the twenty-six suicides occurred in just two of these families.

PART THREE

THE FOUR
PERSPECTIVES OF
DEPRESSION

*Pity the poor patient with a disease whose doctor rejects
the whole notion of disease. . . . Psychodynamic theories
are based on stories not facts . . . nevertheless every person
is a story. For the patient, this is the most crucial fact of
all.*

—Donald Goodwin, M.D.,
Professor of Psychiatry,
University of Kansas

CHAPTER

Dissent in the Ranks

*We are most likely to get angry and excited in our op-
position to some idea when we ourselves are not quite
certain of our own position, and are inwardly tempted
to take the other side.*

—Thomas Mann,
Buddenbrooks (1903)

Stories like those of Nicole, Joann, Peter, and Elizabeth show the usefulness of seeing their potentially devastating affective disorders as treatable diseases. At the same time, they reveal the unique and personal aspects of each of their experiences. In no other field is there more heated debate about which psychiatric perspective to use as a guide in understanding and treating the conditions that fall within its domain.

The fact is that some people have diseases but all have personalities, behaviors, unique life histories, and aspirations. Elements of many different approaches to depression and manic depressive illness can be effective when appropriately applied to different individuals. If you've seen something of yourself or someone you love in the stories of Nicole, Joann, Peter, and Elizabeth, you know better than most that those suffering from depression or manic-depressive illness deserve the best treatments that all of psychiatry can offer.

The Two Camps

Were you a physician newly graduated from medical school and beginning a residency in psychiatry, you would probably be asked whether you were a *biological* psychiatrist—one who "believes in" the use of drugs to treat psychiatric illness—or a *psychodynamic* psychiatrist, one who believes that psychotherapy, sometimes called "talk therapy," is the best treatment for patients. You might be viewed with suspicion by both camps if you hesitated, as many psychiatrists do, to declare an exclusive allegiance to one or the other.

Sigmund Freud was, perhaps, the most famous psychodynamic, or "mind," doctor. His techniques were based largely on the idea that an empathic professional could uncover painful conflicts locked in a patient's unconscious. Once the conflicts were exposed, Freud believed, the patient could deal openly with them and build a healthier life.

While many of Freud's ideas have been disputed, his contribution to the development of formal psychotherapy methods is unquestionable, as is the usefulness of these methods in particular patients with specific problems. In a parallel way, medical therapies targeted at brain structures, such as tricyclic antidepressants and ECT treatment (see Chapters 19 and 20) for depression, can achieve remarkable results when used appropriately. When medical and psychological therapies are used together, both the diseased body and the suffering person should benefit.

Try as one might, any attempt to explain all the possible disruptions in mental life on the basis of either disturbing life events or incapacitating brain disease is impossible. As Paul McHugh and Phillip Slavney have put it:

> Psychiatrists must comprehend and treat patients whose minds are distressed and patients whose brains are diseased; patients whose choices are damaging, and patients whose capacity to choose has been damaged; patients who desire our help and ask for it, and patients who desperately need our help but repudiate it.

The subtlety and promise of psychiatry lies not in choosing the right camp, but in knowing when and in what measure to use the best methods from each.

Attacking on Four Fronts

Different psychiatrists at different times in different medical institutions have viewed affective disorders in different ways. Some have approached them as diseases based on bodily abnormalities. Others have seen in them the reflections of vulnerable personalities. A third group has argued that the root of the problem lies in maladaptive behaviors. Finally, still others have asserted that depression and manic-depressive illness develop from unfortunate life events or choices, the understandable chapters in individual life stories. As we said in the preface to this book, while we have found that recognizing depression and manic-depressive illness as diseases is most illuminating, we believe that all four perspectives are necessary and complementary parts of a complete approach to the ill patient.

The chapters that follow will give you more than just the facts about affective disorders. They will also give you insight into the ways psychiatrists think. Communicating this view of a medical specialty is an ambitious goal. We believe that you will want to know not only what psychiatrists have learned about depression and manic-depressive illness but also how they learned it, how they can best apply it, and how they can learn more.

CHAPTER

The Disease Perspective

> *My first impression was that something had sneaked up*
> *on me. I had no idea I was depressed, that is, mentally.*
> *I knew I felt bad, I knew I felt low. I knew I had no*
> *faith in the work I was doing or the people I was working*
> *with, but I didn't imagine I was sick.*
> —Joshua Logan,
> AMA Symposium on Depression,
> (June 24, 1974)

How Do Physicians Define Disease?

dis·ease (diz-'ēz) *n* **1** *obs*: trouble **2**: a condition of the living animal
or plant body or of one of its parts that impairs the performance
of a vital function: sickness, malady.*

The definition of disease has changed. The "obsolete" definition, trouble, has been replaced by a more modern one—a
bodily condition that impairs how we function. The new definition
describes better how disease limits us, but the defining words
("condition," "impairs," "function") are still imprecise.

The reason such definitions fall short is that disease itself is a
concept, not something tangible. It is easier to recognize concrete
examples, such as diabetes, stroke, and the common cold, than
to grasp the general meaning of disease.

*Webster's Ninth New Collegiate Dictionary, Merriam-Webster Inc., Spring-
field, Mass., 1983.

89

Yet the modern concept of disease has been a very powerful social force (see "It's Illness, Not Weakness," later in this chapter). The concept structures a relationship of sorts between the ill person and the community. This relationship offers the ill person the tremendous resources of the medical establishment (doctors, hospitals, prescription drugs), and it expects, in return, that the person will seek proper treatment and follow medical advice. For those who are considered not only ill but also incapacitated, society accepts and, in some cases, insists that they do not work.

The origins of the word "disease" are literal—meaning "lack of ease"—but the significance of the word has changed. It has become, in modern usage, a framework on which physicians hang clinical information, a powerful way to organize symptoms into familiar categories. A hundred different doctors would be likely to make the same diagnosis in a man complaining of thirst, weight loss, and frequent urination who has sugar detectable in his urine. The most likely diagnosis would be apparent because experience has shown that people with such complaints frequently fit into the category called "diabetes."

As our understanding of biology has improved, explaining an individual's disease has come to require more than the cluster of symptoms a patient reports. We refer to the cluster itself as a *syndrome* and proceed to seek the *pathology*—the bodily abnormality—that underlies it. Thus, we find that in diabetes the syndrome of thirst, weight loss, and excessive urination is due to an elevated blood-sugar level that is sometimes caused by a damaged pancreas which is unable to manufacture the hormone insulin in adequate amounts.

But we don't stop at pathology. We seek the disease's *etiology*, or cause. For diabetes, medical researchers attempt to find what has caused the damage to the pancreas. A genetic defect? A virus? A disorder of the body's immune system? When the answer is known, diagnosing someone as a Type I diabetic will require not only the syndrome that includes thirst, not only the pathology of impaired pancreatic function, but also, perhaps, proof of an inherited defect of the body's immune system. (See Figure 5.)

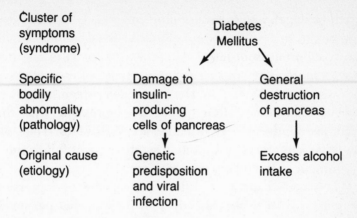

Figure 5. The elements of a disease, here diabetes, from two different injuries.

Even before the etiology of diabetes is known, we are willing to identify patients with the familiar syndrome and pathology as victims of a disease. This is because there are objective signs of diabetes—increased blood sugar being the most prominent.

Only in psychiatry does the use of the word "disease" stir controversy. "Mental illness" is a problematic phrase for many because the first word implies experiences and thoughts—the private lives of individuals—while the second word suggests objective measures that can be applied to the whole population. It is difficult to imagine that something as intensely personal as mental experiences could be tied up in neat categorical packages.

Is Depression a Disease?

In considering whether depression (or manic-depressive illness) is a disease we ask three questions:

1. Does depression constitute a syndrome?

2. Do we know the underlying bodily abnormality (pathology)?

3. Do we understand what causes depression—its etiology?

If we took depression to mean simply low mood, then the answer to each question would be no. But, as already discussed, individuals suffering from major depression have more in common than low mood. They experience a wide range of associated symptoms (see pages 15 to 22). Decreased self-esteem, inability to concentrate, and lack of energy are, to depression, what thirst, weight loss, and excessive urination are to diabetes. They, along with other symptoms, constitute a syndrome that fulfills the first requirement of the disease perspective.

When a psychiatrist identifies the syndrome of depression in a patient, a great deal is already known about that person. It is likely that he or she has family members who also have the syndrome, and alcoholism would not be unexpected in the family tree. The patient is also at increased risk of suicide.

Unlike a person with normal, everyday sadness, the patient is likely to respond to tricyclic antidepressants or to another form of antidepressant therapy.

But what bodily abnormality might be responsible? For the bulk of depressed individuals, the answer is not final, but much evidence has been accumulated. The finding of imbalances of neurotransmitters in patients with depression (see Chapter 4), along with the fact that drugs that alter these chemical equations actually cure depression (see Chapter 19), makes a strong case for a biochemical "pathology."

One area of new research involves the use of positron emission tomography (PET) to study the pathology of depression. PET scanners generate pictures of the brain that not only show its anatomy but also measure glucose utilization, oxygen consumption, and neurotransmitter receptor function. In people with mania and depression, PET scans show abnormal activity in specific brain regions. What's more, it appears that people who have delusions or hallucinations during manic or depressive episodes have different levels of neurotransmitter receptors than those who do not.

In some cases the answer is more specific. Two examples of underlying pathologies occur in stroke and Parkinson's disease.

Of the hundreds of thousands of stroke victims each year in the United States, about 25 percent of those who survive become depressed. While the lasting handicaps caused by strokes may contribute to depression, they do not explain it completely. Studies show that depression is more common in patients with stroke than in patients with similar handicaps resulting from injuries that did not involve the brain. It is injury to the brain itself that seems to play a central role in the pathology of poststroke depression. Supporting this view is the fact that damage to a specific area called the *anterior left-frontal portion* of the brain is more likely to cause severe depression than damage anywhere else (See Figure 3, Chapter 4).

Parkinson's disease, often accompanied by depression, illustrates another pathology. Parkinson's and, probably, the depression that comes with it are caused by the death of nerve cells (*neurons*) in parts of the *basal ganglia*, a region of the brain that influences movement and, it appears, emotion. Not surprisingly, the left basal ganglia is one of the regions of the brain that may be damaged by strokes that cause depression.

We know depression is a syndrome, and we know its pathology in some cases is damage to brain tissue, but what about the etiology of depression—the cause of the damage? For this answer, we categorize the forms of depression as either genetic types or nongenetic types.

For genetic types of depression, the answer may lie with pieces of *deoxyribonucleic acid* (DNA), the genetic material that is passed from generation to generation and determines hereditary characteristics. DNA is organized into forty-six units called *chromosomes*. Chromosomes, in turn, are made up of building blocks called *genes*. In some families in which recurrent manic-depressive illness and depression are common, the same DNA regions are present in every affected family member. These inherited regions, on chromosomes 6, 11, and X, presumably contain genes that cause manic-depressive or depressive disorders in most family members who inherit them (see Figure 6). The effort to pinpoint these genes, and then hopefully to determine how

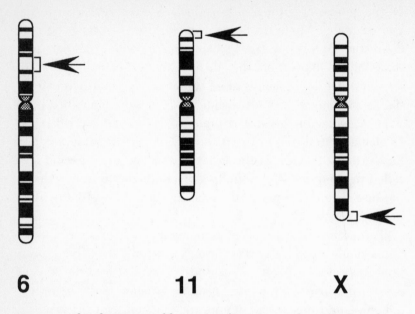

6   **11**   **X**

Figure 6. The chromosomal locations of genetic markers that have been "linked" to manic-depressive and depressive disorders occurring in families. (Adapted from V. A. McKusick, 1986.)

they change brain structure or function, is the goal of much current research.

In nongenetic types of depression, there are various etiologies. For depression associated with stroke, the etiology is usually high blood pressure. For the depression of Parkinson's disease, the etiology may be repeated head trauma or the use of a street drug called MTPT (n-methyl 4-phenyl 1,2,36-tetrahydropyridine). For other cases the etiology is still completely unknown.

What we are finally left with, then, is that depression, a syndrome that includes decreased self-esteem, inability to concentrate, and lack of energy, probably rests on several bodily abnormalities (pathologies) and many etiologies or causes. Syndrome plus pathology plus etiology equals disease. We've satisfied to a great degree the questions we needed to ask before we called depression a disease. That's good news—and bad news.

It's Illness, Not Weakness

No one is to blame. Just as a diabetic cannot, by willpower alone, control his or her blood sugar, a person with depression cannot simply decide to elevate his or her mood. Norman Cousins notwithstanding, it would be foolhardy to depend solely on a mind-over-matter approach to a disease. Knowing this should help release those with depression from the painful suspicion, which some harbor, that what really lies behind their illness is a personal failing or weakness. Personal strength can't, by itself, change the genes a person has inherited or the stroke a person has had.

Seeing depression as a disease could help to remove the prejudice toward psychiatric patients that is cloaked in words like "crazy." While it might be more comfortable for many people to assume that their current good health (or good habits or good sense) protects them from depressive disorders, this is not so. The fact is that everyone is vulnerable to depression. Once it is understood that each of us is a potential victim of this illness, it becomes more difficult to stigmatize those who are actually suffering from it.

The disease perspective also brings tremendous power to bear on developing effective treatments. It was the use of the syndrome-pathology-etiology structure that helped researchers conquer illnesses like smallpox and polio. They identified the symptom complexes common to patients with the illnesses, the underlying bodily abnormalities or pathologies, and, finally, the etiologies— variola virus and poliovirus, respectively. Knowing that viruses were responsible directed researchers toward the development of vaccines that have eliminated smallpox and almost eliminated polio. This same systematized way of thinking about disease will generate fresh ideas for treating or, even better, preventing depressive and other affective disorders.

Even now, available treatments can help the vast majority of people with depression. Tricyclic antidepressants and monoamine oxidase inhibitors, which are thought to work by increasing the available supply of the neurochemical messengers norepinephrine and serotonin, relieve depression in up to 80 percent of depressed individuals. ECT therapy, which involves electrical stimulation of the brain, is successful in up to 90 percent. Even the energy of light has been harnessed in a treatment for one type of depression. These highly effective treatments are described in detail in Chapters 19 and 20.

It's Not a Simple Matter

Depression is a disease. Even with the stiffest of upper lips, having depression means needing treatment, possibly requiring hospitalization, and, in many cases, enduring relapses. While 80 percent of patients respond very well to current treatments, 20 percent do not.

Families should understand that depression is a recurrent illness—more than half of the individuals who are treated successfully once experience depression again. Families should also understand the real risk of suicide in depressed people and the characteristics of those at highest risk (see Chapter 10).

While understanding depression as illness should alleviate the sense that it represents weakness, guilt is not likely to be banished completely. Even though we cannot choose or control which genes we pass on, we may feel badly about passing on to our children a gene that codes for a disease. It is important to remember, however, that any time we reproduce we run the risk of unmasking a variety of disease genes that caused no problem in our own lives. All of us have some of these genes. Moreover, even if we could eliminate the genes that code for affective disorders, we might deprive the world of many talented people. A link between affective disorders and creativity is a subject of current research. It is also worth considering that only a minority of the offspring of a parent with a genetic form of depression or manic-depressive disorder will develop the illness.

Finally, while the disease concept promises advances in the treatment of depression, the concept is not yet fully fleshed out, and direct research is difficult. The brain is the most complex of organs. Even when we know the pathology and etiology that underlie the symptoms of depression, we still do not know how they cause the symptoms—we do not know what physiological processes are involved. What exact chemical or electrical inter-actions, for example, are interrupted when stroke injures the brain or when an abnormal gene causes mania or depression?

Only when this elusive step is understood will we fully com-prehend why our treatments work, that is, what balances they restore. This understanding is critical if we are to advance from treating the symptoms of depression to preventing them from occurring at all.

Illnesses Happen to People

People bring to their experiences with illness a wide range of personality styles and life experiences that influence the way that disease affects them. One person with diabetes might react by dieting, exercising, and closely monitoring his blood sugar. An-other might become despondent and careless in managing his or her life.

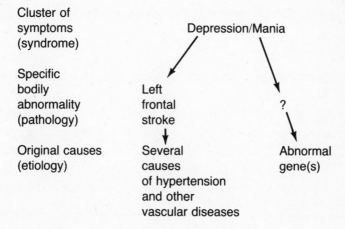

Figure 7. The elements of depression as a disease.

Having described depression as a disease and having detailed the implications, good and bad, of understanding it as such, we must also recognize that there's more to the story. This is because diseases happen to *people*, not just to tissues or organs.

Disease relates to only a particular abnormality and doesn't explain much about the individual as a whole. The disease concept alone cannot bridge the gap. That task is an essential clinical art of the good physician. He or she realizes that treating depression means treating not only a disease but a person.

CHAPTER

The Personality Perspective

It occurred to me that there was no difference between men so profound as the difference between the sick and the well.

—F. Scott Fitzgerald,
The Great Gatsby (1922)

People regularly make observations on each other's personalities or temperaments. The reviews may be neutral, or they may be coupled with a positive ("She's so wonderfully outgoing") or negative ("He's so insecure he makes me nervous") judgment. They also reflect the sense that personality is a relatively constant part of an individual rather than an emotion that comes and goes.

Psychiatrists, too, believe personality is stable. It is described in terms of *traits*—tendencies people demonstrate over and over again to respond to situations in particular ways. Thus, a person who has the characteristic of quickly revealing his or her feelings about situations is considered to be something of an extrovert. A person who is initially quiet and only slowly reveals himself or herself is considered an introvert.

While most people believe that life experiences shape personality, some aspects of personality appear to be inherited. Studies have been done of twins separated after birth and reared apart. The data show that, in spite of different environments, twins still have more personality traits in common than would be expected by chance.

Many traits will be more or less securely rooted in people by the time they reach 30. By then, even with most of life's successes and failures still ahead, an individual responds pretty much as he or she will always respond. People are not textbook examples, however. They vary on a continuous spectrum of personality traits. While there may be living examples of the stereotyped extrovert and introvert, most men and women fall between the extremes.

Ancient physicians believed that a person's temperament was enduring and predetermined. In the opinion of Hippocrates and Galen, two fathers of medicine, personality was decided by the interaction of four bodily fluids—blood, phlegm, yellow bile, and black bile. Depending on which predominated, a person would be either passionate, sluggish, irritable, or depressed, respectively.

Is Depression a Personality Trait?

Some people tend to be chronically unhappy or pessimistic. The melancholy aspect of their personalities seems so pervasive that friends and family label them "depressed." In fact, only about one-third of these demoralized individuals are thought by physicians to be ill. Recall that depression, the clinical illness, is usually episodic. It occurs, disappears, and usually comes back again. Between bouts, people can be their old selves—shy, outgoing, reliable, capricious, driven, laid-back. Some, in fact, swing to the extreme optimism seen in mania. The episodic nature of depressive disorders is quite different from the enduring quality of personality traits. Being a pessimist is not the same as having a depressive illness.

Among chronically discouraged patients, the one-third who are thought to be ill probably suffer from an atypical form of depression (see Chapter 8) that masks their true personalities. Their histories reveal that many have experienced "typical" episodes of severe depression or mild mania in the past. They have many relatives who suffer from depression or mania. Most convincing of all, they often respond to antidepressant medication.

Depression Waiting to Happen

Some physicians believe that people with certain personality types are more vulnerable to illness than others. They might tell a hard-driving executive to "slow down" because they believe that he or she is at increased risk for high blood pressure, heart attack, and the like.

Since depression is a disease, it is therefore reasonable to ask whether particular personality traits could predispose to the illness? If they can, we would expect that certain life circumstances (e.g., tragedy) would trigger the illness in predisposed individuals but not in less vulnerable persons. This commonsense approach to depression was taught by Dr. Adolph Meyer at Johns Hopkins in the early twentieth century. He saw personality as the gunpowder (predisposition), life circumstance as the flame (provocation), and depression as the explosive result.

Indeed, many people with typical depression and mania have a predominant mood which is part of their personalities even when they are well. They might seem always pessimistic, unusually cheerful, or irritable. Others seem to bounce back and forth between cheerful and despondent moods without much provocation. Are the mood components of their personalities predispositions to affective illness?

There is little evidence to indicate that this is so. It would, in fact, be difficult to find a "typical" personality type that could be associated with the likelihood of depression.

This is not to say that people are all equally susceptible to feeling low. It is important, however, to distinguish between low mood and major depression. To be sure, some individuals will become despondent in the face of circumstances that might not bring the same reaction from others. A particularly sensitive person, for example, would be more likely to become terribly sad in response to criticism than a less sensitive person would be.

But it is not at all clear that this kind of "depression" is the same as the illness described in terms of syndrome, pathology, and etiology. We are unsure about this because we lack crucial information about the disease process underlying depression. If we knew more completely the biochemical and anatomic changes that occur in the illness, we might be able to detect similar changes in, for example, sensitive people reacting to criticism. Then again, we might not.

The Pathoplastic Effect

People don't stop being individuals when they become ill. No disease—cancer, diabetes, or depression—wipes the slate clean. What we have learned and continue to learn is that the particular way a person's illness manifests itself is influenced by his or her personality.

The shaping of disease symptoms by personality is sometimes called the *pathoplastic effect*. There are too few modern studies on the effect, but clinical experience suggests that the many different ways in which depressed individuals suffer may be due, in part, to their differing personality traits. Some depressed persons, for example, complain that they cannot banish a terribly troubling thought (obsession) from their minds. Others report that they feel an inner compulsion to repeat a specific behavior, such as hand washing, again and again.

We believe that most depressed people who describe such obsessive-compulsive symptoms usually were somewhat obsessive-compulsive to begin with. They may, for example, have always felt the need to be unusually neat. Similarly, those people with depression who describe an irrational fear of cancer may have tended to be more health conscious when well than are other persons.

Concentrating exclusively on a problem such as an obsession or a new health concern related to personality can obscure the underlying disease. It is crucial to remember that illness exaggerates the personality trait and turns it into a symptom. Prompt and effective treatment of the depression will return the person to his or her usual, if not problem-free, personality.

Not only the symptoms of illness but also the way a person deals with the symptoms can be influenced by personality. Thus, some cancer patients eventually cope well with their pathology, while others who have the same bodily abnormality are very preoccupied with it.

Depression is no different. When you've seen one, you haven't seen 'em all. The extent to which an individual copes with depression and cooperates with treatment is almost certainly influenced by his or her underlying personality. Probably the most important factor is where the depressed person, when well, would fall on the spectrum between dependence and independence.

People at the two extremes seem to have the hardest time. The overly dependent person may tend to use his or her illness as a perpetual excuse for faltering socially. He or she might also lean too heavily on the hospital or the psychiatrist, not struggling independently to cope with stress and lead a productive life. On the other hand, an overly independent person who falls victim to depression might resist treatment altogether. Physicians, for example, are notoriously difficult patients. Some, when ill, are unable to accept the fact that they need help.

Whereas personality weaknesses can make treating and overcoming depression more difficult, personality strengths can make things easier. Patients who do not have a significant tendency toward either extreme of the dependence-independence spectrum, for instance, are most willing to follow medical advice. While this might seem like nothing more than good sense, it actually takes a great deal of personal fortitude to overcome the lethargy and hopelessness of depression in order to work with one's psychiatrist.

Where Depression Ends and the Person Begins

When a physical illness such as cancer is treated, patients can often see a lump disappearing or a lesion healing. There is little question that the bodily abnormality was a foreign invader, not a normal part of the person. It wasn't there before the individual got sick, and it should be gone when he or she is well. In psychiatric illness, on the other hand, the boundaries between the normal parts of the person and those that represent illness are less clear. Patients who are successfully treated for depression often wonder whether some of their emotions are manifestations of their healthy personalities or symptoms of their illness. Sometimes they need to relearn who they are—where their depressions stop and they themselves begin.

Usually the question doesn't come up with severe symptoms of depression, such as hopelessness, inability to sleep, or drastically decreased self-esteem. Just like a person with heart disease who experiences the return of crushing chest pain, a depressed person will usually identify the classic symptoms of depression as illness.

The gray zone includes feelings like mild irritability and transient sadness. Indeed, not only the post-depressive individual but his or her family and friends can be so vigilant for a relapse that they become anxious with any show of emotion. All involved need to be aware that a full range of emotions is normal and desirable in persons successfully treated for depression or mania. Although painful, relearning what is illness and what is not may take a great deal of time.

The confidants of the recovered person need to find a way to reassure themselves about the health of their friend or family member without being alarming. Depending on the situation, they might voice their concern as a request to the recovered person for guidance in judging his or her behavior. It can be frustrating and disconcerting if the person feels that none of his or her emotions are being accepted as healthy and genuine.

Not even a psychiatrist can know in an instant whether a momentary emotion is a manifestation of illness. The judgment is better made in the context of the entire pattern of the person's recent emotional responses. An isolated event will be more alarming if it keeps company with other symptoms of the syndrome, such as decreased energy, lack of concentration, or impaired sleep.

As difficult as it can be for successfully treated individuals to relearn that the person and the illness are not one and the same, it is even more difficult for those still in the throes of a depressive episode. Many people will accept their depression as illness only when they are well. When they experience a relapse, they lose this insight and once again see the depression as just another indication of their flawed personalities.

Individuals with some reserve of energy left can be very persuasive on this point. One of our patients, a retired businessman, became very depressed and worried excessively about his financial affairs. Although he was extremely successful, he became convinced that he had not accrued a sufficient fortune to leave to his heirs. He focused on a period twenty years earlier, when he had argued unsuccessfully with his partners for a major business expansion. If only he had been more cynical about their judgment, he felt, his children's futures would be secure. He was just too trusting.

In fact, the patient's family and business associates attributed his remarkable success in nearly all his undertakings to his ability to work closely with partners. Their teamwork, based on the trust he inspired, had guided his company through a string of successes. But no argument from us or from his family and friends could convince him that he was viewing himself with a negative bias— a bias caused by illness.

It is essential that family members and others recognize such self-criticism as a symptom of depression. Treating the underlying illness, not engaging in personality analyses, is the best treatment for this type of negative self-attitude.

The Personality Perspective at Its Best

The personality perspective alone fails as a complete explanation of depression. Depressed people are not "just like that." They have an illness.

As we said at the close of the last chapter, however, treating depression means treating a person, not just a disease. The personality traits that shape temperament when a person is well can also influence his or her symptoms when the person is ill. Recognizing the personality behind the pathology helps psychiatrists understand why specific symptoms predominate in certain individuals. It also allows some prediction about which persons are likely to become attached to the patient role and which will reject the idea that they are sick at all. Finally, it is the personality perspective that psychiatrists employ when helping patients and their families understand where depression ends and they or their loved ones begin.

The idea that the perspectives of psychiatry (here, disease and personality) work with, not against, each other is one that will be echoed in the chapters ahead. It is in the synergy between disease, personality, behavior, and life experiences that the unique faces of depressive disease take shape, and it is there that the answers to depression must be found.

CHAPTER

The Behavior Perspective

I remember the rage I used to feel when a prediction went awry. I could have shouted at the subjects of my experiments, "Behave, damn you, behave as you ought."
—B. F. Skinner,
Walden Two (1961)

"He Just Acts Like That"

In behavioral experiments, rats are often trained to perform tasks in order to obtain rewards. A pellet of food, for example, might drop within the rat's reach only after the rat has pressed a lever at one side of the cage. In a short time, the rat learns the connection between pressing the lever and obtaining food and can even be taught to press a specific number of times in order to obtain a reward. The rat's behavior in pressing the lever is more than the random activity of his muscles. The activity has a specific goal behind it—the acquisition of food.

This goal-directed quality is the hallmark of behavior and separates it from simple activity. It allows us to understand what a particular behavior means to an individual, what outcome he or she hopes it might bring. When a mother says of her sobbing son, "He's just doing it for the attention," she is theorizing about what her son's behavior means in the context of his individual circumstances.

107

Looking at behavior in terms of the anticipated outcomes is only one vantage point. We might instead look inward and examine the drives that motivate behavior. For a rat in his cage, hunger drives his interest in obtaining food. For human beings, who interact in a complex social world, the drives that inform goals range from biological (sexual appetite and the cyclical appetites for activity and sleep) to sociological (the desire for recognition and the need to create). Moreover, while some goals are obvious to the person trying to achieve them, others are subtle or even unconscious.

Some people would focus less on the idea that we are passive hostages to drives and goals we do not understand and more on the belief that we are free to choose our behaviors. They might say that some individuals drink excessively because they choose to do so, not because they need to do so, or that some pine for lost loves because they choose martyrdom. No cages and levers for them.

As is so often the case, the most informed view of behavior may be the least exclusive. Behaviors grow out of both drives and free choice. Often a mixture of the two is behind any one behavior. An example can be found in the behavior of eating. All human beings feel hunger (a drive) and perform various activities (hunting, harvesting, cooking, shopping, importing) to achieve the goal of obtaining food. But, as human beings, we make choices about acceptable ways of satisfying our hunger. Different cultures identify different items as food. What we eat, when we eat, and how we eat are shaped by the mores of our society.

The consequences of violating those mores will also influence the way we behave in the future. If we ignore social custom and publicly eat food without using the proper utensils, for example, we will be subject to disapproving glances. We might even be asked to leave a restaurant.

Could depression be a behavioral strategy in the service of specific goals and driven by specific needs? Do we simply need to teach people to choose better strategies to cope in society? Physicians who study learned helplessness theory, cognitive theory, and motivated behavior have offered explanations for depression that, at first glance, seem to answer yes.

The Learned Helplessness Theory

People will go to great lengths to escape emotional pain. They might change jobs, start or end relationships, or move from one coast to another. Their attempts to put themselves at peace with themselves and their environments can consume tremendous energy.

Experiments with animals have raised the possibility of a limit to the escape response. In one experiment, researchers placed dogs in cages in which one-half of the floor was equipped to deliver electric shocks. After a number of jolts, the dogs jumped a barrier from the electrified to the nonelectrified part of the cage. In the next phase of the experiment, however, a harness prevented the dogs from jumping to the safe side. No amount of energy they expended would stop the shocks. The unexpected result was that once they had experienced pain for long enough, the dogs ceased trying to jump the barrier—even when the harnesses were removed. They passively accepted the shocks.

Learned helplessness, as it is called, has been theorized to explain depression. Its proponents believe that depressed people have accepted that no strategy to remove the turmoil in their lives will be of any use. In the face of seemingly inescapable emotional pain, they become paralyzed. The withdrawal, decreased energy, and difficulty in concentrating that characterize depression are manifestations of accepting a loss of control over one's environment.

While learned helplessness as the cause of depression does have some intuitive appeal, it takes a real leap of faith to extrapolate from dogs jumping in cages to people interacting in the world. While it would be difficult to completely disprove the connection, there also isn't much data to support it. Does a dog's seeming apathy in the face of physical pain really explain the decreased self-esteem and negativism (see Chapter 1) that characterize the depressed person? Does it shed light on the recurrent, sometimes cyclical, nature of depression? How about the cases in which depression alternates with mania? The cases in which it runs in families? How does learned helplessness explain the dramatic positive effects of medical treatment?

Like other intuitive ways of looking at depression, the learned helplessness theory fails to provide an adequate explanation. What it does offer is a reminder that feelings of helplessness are indeed a prominent feature of the illness (recall the personal accounts in Chapter 5).

These feelings are often expressed. Depressed people share their dismal outlooks with others and, thus, may contribute to their own isolation. No one likes a doomsayer. Isolation, in turn, reinforces their self-images as helpless and hopeless. Psychiatrists can intervene (with the patient's consent) to guide family members to remain supportive in the face of the pessimism and self-blame of their loved one.

To a lesser extent, psychiatrists may counsel the depressed person to relate better to family and friends in order to maintain, not undermine, their support. This is a tall order, since it calls on psychiatrists to "teach" optimism to a person whose illness often includes seemingly impenetrable hopelessness.

The Cognitive Theory

When people become hopeless, perhaps questioning their abilities to succeed socially or professionally, the first response of family and friends is often, "Think positively." Inherent in the advice is the belief that a negative mind-set can perpetuate a person's low mood and contribute to failure.

The *cognitive theory* of depression is a more complex version of this reasoning. Depression is seen as the outgrowth of negative thinking habits that are learned, perhaps beginning in childhood. The death of a parent, the loss of a sibling, or even separation from childhood friends who move far away predisposes the future depressed patient to think negatively—to view losses as irrevocable and uncontrollable. Things just never seem to work out, no matter how hard the person tries. Later in life a loss or defeat that most of us might view as temporary is seen as devastating, and depression sets in.

An example might be a man, made vulnerable by early life experiences, who is deserted by his wife. Most men would be deeply affected by such a turn of events, but they would recruit other family members and friends as support. They might become resentful and angry, but, in time, they would fill the void in their lives with substitutes—work, other relationships, or new hobbies.

Our negative thinker, however, exaggerates his wife's departure. He remembers her as his only source of joy and concludes that life without her will be devoid of any happiness. He cannot formulate an active strategy to resolve his grief. Friends and family, he believes, will surely side with his wife and shun him. The children will live with her and never speak to him. Finally, he begins to question himself. He thinks he is unmanly, incapable of being loved, a poor father, and a terrible husband. He is only one step away from losing his energy, his desire for food, and any remnant of his self-esteem.

All from having learned to think negatively. If psychiatrists could just help their patients adopt a more balanced view of themselves and the world, the theory says, their patients' depressions would lift.

A start could be made by assuring patients that their feelings of hopelessness are symptomatic of illness, not personal weakness. This could be shown by demonstrating their abilities to complete a simple task at home. Even small successes might help break down the walls of pessimism and self-doubt.

It is true that many people with depression respond positively to clear-cut personal success. Psychiatrists might indeed be able to make use of that responsiveness. But the idea that depression is caused by learning a negative mind-set has little experimental evidence behind it. What's more, the theory does not explain the mounting evidence for a neurochemical and genetic role in the etiology of depression.

Like the learned helplessness theory, the cognitive theory leaves unaddressed the cyclical nature of manic-depressive illness. If depressed people are lifelong negative thinkers, why do their depressions come and go, often seasonally? Why does the negative thinking sometimes alternate with the inappropriately positive self-regard of mania?

A Role for Motivation

Both learned helplessness and the cognitive theory are concerned with learned behaviors. They maintain that the depressed person is educated to the fact that no strategy to control his or her world seems to work.

Other behaviors, called *motivated behaviors*, are as much automatic as learned. They are associated with intrinsic needs that our biologies call on us to satisfy. We eat (or at least desire food) when we are starved. When we emerge into sexual maturity, we seek mates in order to reproduce and preserve ourselves.

Could depression be a set of motivated behaviors meant to conserve energy, a human equivalent of hibernation? We are, after all, animals. And depression does often cycle with the seasons. Recalling the sleep of bears in caves, some theorists propose that the fatigue and decreased activity seen in depression are parts of a biologically driven strategy to decrease our need for calories and preserve precious resources.

The idea that a need to conserve energy is a part of depression highlights the fact that exercise, perhaps by stimulating the release of certain brain neurotransmitters, does help many affected individuals. Alcohol, on the other hand, acting as a central nervous system depressant, makes matters worse.

Like the other behavioral theories, however, equating depression with hibernation is an incomplete explanation. First, although some depressions are seasonal, most are not. Second, depressed people are plagued by more than fatigue and lack of interest in activities. They suffer with decreased self-esteem and, often, suicidal ideation. Finally, the need to cyclically conserve energy, if present in human beings, would be an evolutionary remnant (like the appendix)—a throwback. We would want to seek the cause of the defect in those afflicted.

The search would bring us back to the disease perspective. Perhaps a damaged or missing gene would be found that in normal individuals suppresses the vestigial need. Or maybe those with the need would be found to have other physiological abnormalities that actually make it necessary, at certain times, for them to conserve energy in this distorted way.

The Behavior Perspective at Its Best

The fact that our exploration of depression and behavior brings us back to the disease perspective might make a good deal of sense. Disease can cause profound changes in behavior. Evidence from the laboratory, in fact, shows that lesions in specific areas of the brain can diminish an animal's ability to seek reward and avoid punishment. Conversely, chemical stimulants and antidepressants injected into these areas cause an animal to work toward rewards more actively.

Although behavioral explanations alone seem to leave key questions unanswered, each has a role in the understanding of depression. The most obvious link between abnormal behavior and depression is suicide. But short of this most tragic behavior, depressed people do often get into the habit of thinking negatively. They also benefit from demonstrated successes. Certain behaviors (like exercise) may indeed help to diminish their fatigue, while others (including drinking alcohol) will only make matters worse. Moreover, once harmful behaviors are born during depression, they can acquire a life of their own, requiring continued treatment even after the depression has resolved. (See pages 57–60.)

We look forward to more productive behavioral research in the future. The elegance with which the behavior and disease perspectives intersect underscores our belief that a complete understanding of depression will require the best of each perspective of psychiatry.

CHAPTER

The Life Story Perspective

*In the middle of the journey of our life I came to myself
within a dark wood where the straight way was lost.*
—Dante Alighieri,
The Divine Comedy (c. 1310–1320)

A well-written life is almost as rare as a well-spent one.
—Thomas Carlyle,
Critical and Miscellaneous Essays (1827)

Every Person Is a Story

Even with the information on depression provided by our knowledge of disease, personality, and behavior, we would still be lacking in our understanding of the illness. This is because these three perspectives do not fully illuminate the depressed individual as a human being. They do not speak to the unique set of life experiences that can color not only a person's symptoms but also his or her way of interpreting those symptoms and responding to them. While the lives of Nicole, Joann, and Peter (see Chapter 5) share some striking similarities, their accounts read as three different stories because they describe three different people.

The *life story perspective* speaks to this need to understand the depressed person as an individual in distress. In so doing, it asks questions very different from those of the disease perspective. When we view a psychiatric condition as a disease, we ask what pathology (bodily abnormality) has caused the condition. The basic question is, How did the illness came about? For a given individual with major depression, we might occasionally find the answer is brain injury caused by a stroke or by use of the drug MTPT. In life story reasoning, the question is not how but *why*. Why has the person's life taken a turn into Dante's dark wood?

Answering the "why" question requires that the psychiatrist and the patient work to compose a biography of the patient's experiences (sometimes recent, sometimes long past) in a way that helps in understanding the person's present state. The goal is to discover meaningful connections between events, relationships, or emotions in a patient's life and his or her symptoms. The life story that results describes in a coherent way a human being in constant flux. It takes brushstrokes from the person's life and puts them together in a complete portrait. Again, this synthesis is different from the disassembly of a disease into syndrome, pathology, and etiology.

What the life story perspective shares with the disease perspective is its persuasive power. A well-written life story can be a very convincing way for both patient and physician to understand problems in psychiatry. It speaks to the empathic understandings all of us, psychiatrists and laypersons alike, develop regarding how a vulnerable individual can be destabilized by stressful events.

Nothing Can Resist Empathic Understanding

A complete appreciation of the disease perspective, with its framework of syndrome, pathology, and etiology, calls for training in the natural sciences. This is because using the perspective clinically requires not only certain tools (data analysis, strict classification of symptoms, laboratory testing, neuropharmacology) but also extensive knowledge of specific cause-and-effect relationships that are not intuitive. Without a knowledge of brain anatomy and function, there is nothing intuitively obvious about the fact that patients with strokes in the anterior left-frontal portion of the brain are at greatest risk for depression. The fact doesn't shake us and make us say, "Of course he's depressed! Anyone would be."

The life story perspective delivers the lock-and-key fit of *intuition*. When a psychiatrist writes a story that explains a patient's depression as the result of a frustrated career plan or another failed relationship, he or she can relate to it on a basic, human level. The psychiatrist can see why event X led to emotion Y. In essence, the physician imagines how low he or she would feel if he or she were in the distressed person's shoes. The psychiatrist empathizes.

Some part of the ability to appreciate the suffering of others may be innate, but all of us are also trained to use the life story perspective. As children, we listen to adults interpret our own behavior as the understandable outgrowth of our life experiences. When a father explains his popular daughter's sadness at losing a class election by saying, "It's very difficult for her, she's not used to losing," it is the life story perspective at work. We all write "why" stories about the people in our lives.

Some stories might seem obvious, while others, involving unconscious motivations and intentions, would be invisible to the untrained eye. When used by psychiatrists with professional training in psychotherapy, however, the life story perspective can be very illuminating indeed. A "why" story, in fact, can be written to explain just about anything. Nothing can resist empathic understanding. It is this sense of universal applicability that at once gives the life story perspective its power and its potential for harm.

Stories Have Authors

Just as historical interpretations by Karl Marx and Adam Smith draw on the same body of facts to support two very different views of economic development, two psychiatrists may formulate widely divergent life stories to explain depression in the same patient. The therapist's own life experiences and preconceptions flavor the way he or she sifts through the totality of a patient's experiences, identifying some as critical to the problem at hand and others as distracting or irrelevant. There are even institutional and regional tendencies of interpretation that will influence how a particular psychiatrist views a given patient's distress.

No absolutely objective standard exists for judging which story is correct and which misses the mark. Instead, we rely on the physician's and patient's beliefs that the explanation accounts for the present state of affairs.

Persuasion plays a large role in this. A proficient clinician will recruit the patient into the drama he or she is constructing not necessarily because it is historically accurate but because it is well enunciated and forcefully presented. Nevertheless, the edited account that results might still be useful if it is convincing enough to serve as a path out of Dante's dark wood.

The danger arises when the life story perspective is inappropriate for the particular psychiatric problem at hand. Nothing in the method alerts the therapist to when it should be abandoned. Unlike the disease model, resting on physical science that can be tested, life stories can be supported by any observation and cannot be refuted by any test. A patient's depression or mania may go on unchecked as the therapist pursues the course of life story reasoning into increasingly troubled waters.

This is a concern because the life story perspective never completely explains depression or manic-depressive illness. It often illuminates the particular content of depressed thoughts— why, for example, one depressed person dwells on her ineptitude in business while another dwells on his lack of integrity in relationships—but it does not shed light on the form depressed beliefs and perceptions take, such as delusions and hallucinations. It does not explain how it is that the illness runs in families that share particular regions of DNA, that injury to specific areas of the brain causes it, and that antidepressant medications seem to stop it.

The seductiveness, the intuitiveness, of life story reasoning should not monopolize the therapist's view of depression. If used exclusively, this reasoning deprives the patient of effective treatments that come from other perspectives, such as the disease model. It can also deprive the patient of a view of his or her condition as illness rather than personal weakness, as misfortune rather than failure.

"It Isn't Depression, It's Burnout"

Some people constantly compose autobiographies; they mentally write their own life stories. The plot of each is affected by how the author feels physically and emotionally. Whether we write ourselves as heroes or villains, winners or losers, saints or scoundrels, therefore, changes over time.

When people fall victim to depression, they write chapters that explain where the sadness, fatigue, loss of interest in activities, or decreased appetite are coming from. Typically, they decide that it is coming from within—that something is inherently wrong with them as people. This harsh introspection initiates or exacerbates the decreased self-attitude that is one of the hallmarks of the illness.

The chapters are read in many places, but one important place is in the therapist's office. Once the patient presents intuitive explanations for his or her symptoms, the psychiatrist may find it difficult to resist the temptation to build on them. In the search for meaningful connections between events and emotions in a patient's life, the psychiatrist can become the coauthor of a story that rests on the patient's injured self-esteem.

One of our patients, who we'll call Jonathan, constructed an elaborate life story to explain why, for five years, he had experienced terrible lows and exhilarating highs that alternated exactly every twenty-four hours. So regular was the cycle, in fact, that he could predict his "good" days and "bad" days three months in advance.

Jonathan was a hospital administrator who had sought help

from many specialists, including a psychiatrist, without relief. The problem, he finally theorized, was simply that he had become bored with his job—all the regulations and labor problems. His boredom brought the bad days, when he either would call in sick, unable to get out of bed, or would hide away in a distant office, hopeful that subordinates would carry the load. He stopped eating. He felt lazy and terribly guilty. "It isn't depression," he said, "it's burnout."

But if boredom brought the bad days, what, we asked, about the seemingly too-good days, when he would arrive at the office early and stay late, completing task after task without a hint of boredom or exhaustion? What about the dates after work when he would dance until the morning? Simple, he explained. After a day of loafing, he felt so guilty that he worked tirelessly to make up for the lost day's work. He could do anything.

It all made perfect sense to Jonathan, but not to us. In his swings of mood, we saw not boredom alternating with normal guilt, but classic symptoms of rapid-cycling manic-depressive illness. We prescribed a combination of the drugs lithium and nortriptyline (see Chapter 19), and Jonathan has not experienced an episode of depression or mania in four years.

Many cases of manic-depressive illness are more subtle than Jonathan's. They lack the clear periodicity of highs and lows that he lived with for so long. We chose Jonathan's story because, even with the extreme regularity of his mood shifts, the idea that an illness really could be the explanation took him by surprise. He hadn't thought of the possibility, because he had not been educated to interpret his symptoms as those of a disease. (Neither had the specialists he had consulted previously.) After all, for years he had read newspaper stories linking the "breakdowns" or suicides of famous men and women to anything from job stress to troubled childhoods. Few had talked about illness lurking in the background. To Jonathan, chest pain might mean heart attack and joint stiffness might mean arthritis, but alternating lows and highs meant simply that he was a bored or guilty person. He was doing life story reasoning without all the facts.

The Life Story Perspective at Its Best

Anyone who has confronted a serious health problem will agree that illness itself has been a dramatic chapter in his or her life story. Disease hurts, frightens, isolates, scars, and challenges its victims. Helping a person with depression requires attention not only to the waxing and waning of symptoms with various treatments, but also to the impact of experiencing emotional pain, hospitalization, and interruption of work or education. This is no place for syndrome, pathology, and etiology. It is the domain of empathy. Only through life story reasoning can the impact of experiencing an illness—and, sadly, one with some social stigma—be understood and softened.

The story a therapist writes to understand what depression means to an affected individual should be different for each person because people are different. They come to illness with a host of preconceptions and expectations. Some people will try to understand their depression as simple misfortune, while others will interpret it religiously as punishment from God for past sins. Still others might recall a relative who passed away from a brain tumor and believe that they are on the same path.

For a physical illness, the stories are complicated enough. But for depression, the stories will likely be entwined with the patients' symptoms (especially decreased self-attitude), making some people identify themselves as evil, others as impotent. Intervening, then, requires that the therapist recognize the subtleties of the life story that the patient is writing for himself or herself. Like that of our patient Jonathan, it is likely to be written without all the facts.

As we said at the beginning of this book, knowledge is power. When the facts about depression and disease are in hand, the story a patient writes can change dramatically. Recall the words of our patient Joann from Chapter 5:

> At a time when my life was bleakest, my therapist finally convinced me to see another doctor. It was a very hard thing for me to do. Although the therapist told me that I might have a

depression, I had never heard of any such illness. I thought that
if such an illness really did exist, it would have to be pretty rare.
I didn't believe that I could be lucky enough to have a real illness,
with a name, characterized by the symptoms I had been experiencing. . . . If he said that I didn't have the illness called
depression, there would be no other way out but to commit
suicide.

The message is that life story reasoning at its best is complementary, not contradictory, to the disease concept. The perspectives
of psychiatry are parts of a whole that, taken together, hold the
greatest promise of bringing the depressed person out from the
dark wood.

16

Bringing the Four Perspectives Together

It would be a great thing to understand pain in all its meanings.

> —Peter Mere Latham (1789–1875)
> *Collected Works*, Book I

A United Front

When we introduced the perspectives of psychiatry, we talked of them as a strategy to attack depression on four fronts. We explained that psychiatrists at different institutions and at different times have seen in depression the manifestations of a disordered biology, personality, behavioral strategy, or life story. Even when psychiatrists agree that more than one perspective is enlightening, there are still different approaches to integrating the biological, psychological, and social aspects of human emotional problems.

What should be clear from the preceding chapters is that, at their best, the four approaches complement, rather than contradict, each other. With the disease perspective at the helm, they blend into a single united front.

Take, for example, a 30-year-old man named Robert, who is experiencing a severe episode of depression. Employing the disease perspective would, perhaps, alert us to the classic syndrome of decreased self-esteem, inability to concentrate, and lack of energy. It would prompt us to ask whether he has suffered from depression in the past and whether he has ever experienced symptoms of mania. We would want to explore whether Parkinson's disease or another associated physical condition such as stroke might be involved. Knowing the genetic heritage of depression, we would inquire whether other family members have experienced intense highs or lows. We could predict, to an extent, the probable course of Robert's illness, including the likelihood of relapses. And we could prescribe treatment to shorten the current episode and ward off future episodes.

As we begin to meet with Robert, family members might describe him as overly dependent on them, unwilling to accept responsibility, and hesitant to accept social challenges. While we would caution the family to hold final judgments about Robert's disposition until his depression clears, we would keep in mind the possibility that we are working with a person with a dependent personality. We might need to take special care to ensure that he does not use our diagnosis as an excuse to avoid independence once he is well.

Robert's parents might alert us a week later to their son's worrisome consumption of alcohol, a behavior that never seemed to be a problem before depression took hold. Great emphasis would need to be placed on controlling his drinking not only during antidepressant treatment but after treatment is completed.

Finally, Robert might confide that his lack of energy and inability to concentrate really mean that he must be dissatisfied with his upcoming marriage. We would point out that he is doing life story reasoning without the facts—that, while he might be unhappy with his relationship, his symptoms are those of an illness that might temporarily cloud his view of his marriage.

A Complex Weave

As Robert's case demonstrates, the diagnosis and treatment of depression is a fabric woven from interlacing perspectives. Far from competing, these sustain and color each other.

Each of the four perspectives has its own general formula for solving patients' problems: The disease perspective would prescribe a treatment to remove an abnormal body part or to repair damaged body functions. The personality perspective would make the troubled person aware of personal strengths and weaknesses and would direct him or her to "play" the strengths and avoid the weaknesses. The behavior perspective would attempt to extinguish injurious behaviors and reinforce healthy behaviors. Finally, the life story perspective would help a troubled person see his or her situation and choices more clearly and accept the consequences of the choices.

We believe that psychiatrists will, more and more, find the disease approach to be the most useful perspective for understanding depressive and manic syndromes. This is due less to its intuitive appeal than to its practical appeal. The exciting pace at which the disease perspective will continue to uncover the basis for, and treatment of, depression makes it a powerful blueprint.

The pace, in fact, has never been quicker. It is now clear that the disease perspective has yielded only a fraction of what it promises in the future. Thinking in terms of syndrome, pathology, and etiology is likely to lead to the recognition of several different types of depression that will direct us to even more effective, tailored treatments.

It was the very same insistence on identifying syndrome, pathology, and etiology that, under the leadership of Sir William Osler (1849–1919) of Johns Hopkins, took medical education from the world of apprenticeships in therapeutic cults to the world of basic and clinical sciences. He emphasized that treatment be based on the physiological underpinnings of recognized patterns of symptoms, and we have reaped the benefits of this dictum. Everything from antibiotics to the first treatments for AIDS owes something to Osler's well-conceived foundation.

The point of discovery at which psychiatry is poised is that each perspective, at its best, enriches the disease model that has served so well. Just as Osler spoke of the infinite hues with which personality and life experience colored common medical disorders, we recognize that, on a canvas of illness, the portrait of depression is painted from a palette of perspectives.

What Are You Treating?

A favorite line of senior physicians questioning those caring for patients with multiple medical problems is, "What are you treating with that drug?" The question usually arises when a new antibiotic has been added to a patient's drug regimen without a clear-cut rationale.

Answering the question requires knowing what bacterium is responsible for the patient's infection. It presumes that the doctor should have a clear idea of how a drug interferes with the cascade of syndrome, pathology, and etiology. Where does it throw a wrench into the gears of illness?

The preceding chapters, by explaining the way physicians think, have prepared you to understand far more about the treatment of depression than just what works and what doesn't. They should have given you a more critical eye—a tendency to ask "What are you treating?"

This is an essential posture when you consider that some disorders of mood, though extremely distressing, are quite different from major depression and fail to respond to its remedies. Moreover, many less obviously related conditions interact with depression in complex ways. Thus, portraits of the alcoholic, the bulimic, and the compulsive gambler may be colored to some extent by depressive illness.

PART FOUR

CURRENT
TREATMENTS

I believe that depression is terrifying; and elation—its non-identical twin sister—is even more terrifying, attractive as she may be for the moment. . . . However, I'm sure that the thing that is almost as much or more of a menace to the world today is the stupid, almost dogged ignorance of these illnesses; the vast lack of knowledge that they are able to be treated and the seeming ease of the cure, the simplicity of bringing them under control.
　　　　　　　　　—Joshua Logan,
　　　　　　　　　　AMA Symposium on Depression,
　　　　　　　　　　(June 24, 1974)

CHAPTER

The Treatment Plan

*. . . You cannot fail to see that scientific thought is not
an accompaniment or condition of human progress, but
human progress itself.*

—William Kingdom Clifford (1845–1879),
Aims and Instruments of Scientific Thought

The wide variety of effective treatments for affective disorders makes us truly optimistic about the chances for patients to become symptom-free. When accurately diagnosed and competently treated, 80 percent of patients with depression or mania go into complete remission. For those who need it, maintenance treatment can usually prevent relapses or, at least, decrease their severity and duration.

Diagnosis

Diagnosis is the critical starting point of any treatment plan. It begins by interviewing the patient and others (usually family members) in order to obtain a *history* that includes current symptoms, present medications, past symptoms and illnesses, and family background. The diagnosis of affective disorder is strongly supported when:

1. The patient is presently experiencing sufficient symptoms to fulfill the DSM-III criteria (see Chapter 3, and Figures 1 and 2). Diagnosis is further supported if one or more of the following three items are applicable.

2. Other family members are known to have suffered from depressive or manic symptoms. This is called a *positive family history.*

3. The patient has a past history of medical conditions that can cause or precipitate affective syndromes (stroke, recent childbirth, steroid medications, etc.).

4. The patient has a past history of episodes of depressive or manic symptoms.

Most cases of depressive and manic-depressive disorders can be confidently diagnosed by a psychiatrist who examines the patient and takes the history. When a patient is suffering from unusual symptoms or has trouble describing symptoms, it may take several visits to determine whether or not a depressive (or manic) syndrome is present.

Laboratory Tests

One development that would improve the certainty with which psychiatrists can diagnose affective disorders would be laboratory tests. To be useful, these tests would have to yield results in depressed or manic patients that were reliably different from the norm.

Currently there is no easily interpreted and generally available laboratory test to confirm or rule out the diagnoses of major depressive or manic syndromes. Several tests have, however, been studied and found to be helpful in lending support to a clinician's suspicion that his or her patient suffers from a depressive syndrome. These tests currently are most useful in hospitalized patients with uncertain diagnoses. The laboratory must be specially standardized for this specific purpose.

With these important limitations in mind, there may be occasions before or during treatment for depression when the psychiatrist may perform what is called a *dexamethasone suppression test*. This involves giving a synthetic version of a normal hormone called cortisol and seeing if the body responds appropriately by decreasing its own production of cortisol. Hospitalized patients with severe major depression are more likely than others to show "nonsuppression"—a failure to regulate cortisol production.

Another test is the *sleep electroencephalogram* (EEG), which measures brain electrical activity. In patients with major depression, there is a tendency for the rapid-eye-movement (REM) phase of sleep, during which dreaming occurs, to begin sooner than normal after falling asleep. This test may take up to three nights, with the patient sleeping in a specialized laboratory. It is, therefore, quite expensive and not available in many locations.

Neither of these two tests rules out the presence of major depression. They are, at this stage of their development, useful (and still of limited benefit) in supporting the clinical diagnosis— the diagnosis a psychiatrist reaches through interviewing and examining the patient and taking a complete patient and family history.

Treatment

Once a diagnosis of an affective disorder (or probable affective disorder) is made, a psychiatrist then proposes a treatment plan. An essential skill of today's psychiatrist is to tailor the treatment to the patient. Just as those with high blood pressure may respond to one antihypertensive and not another, depressed patients may be helped more by one particular therapy than another.

The maze of treatment alternatives may seem bewildering. The psychiatrist can clarify the substantial but complicated evidence about which strategies benefit which patients and what outcomes (i.e, prognoses) can be expected with and without treatments. Science is taking its rightful place beside the art of psychiatry.

18

CHAPTER

Psychotherapy

*No themes are so human as those that reflect for us, out
of the confusion of life, the close connection of bliss and
bale, of the things that help with the things that hurt,
so dangling before us forever that bright hard medal, of
so strange an alloy, one face of which is somebody's right
and ease and the other somebody's pain and wrong.*
—Henry James,
    Prefaces to *What Maisie Knew* (1907–1909)

The Role of Psychotherapy

While there are many different kinds of psychotherapy, all forms
involve a confiding relationship between a professional therapist
and a patient that allows the patient's experiences and predica-
ments to be shared. The hope is that by better understanding his
or her emotions and behavior, the patient will be able to tailor
successful emotional, social, and even professional strategies. As
Drs. McHugh and Slavney have written, "Psychotherapy aims to
enable the self to be a more effective director of the life plan."

Most psychotherapies are derived from the life story perspective, with its theories of human development and human
suffering. Psychoanalysis, for example, concentrates on traumatic
experiences during one's earliest years. It is during infancy, psychoanalysts believe, that the roots of many adult problems take
hold. Other psychotherapies, however, are based on another, or

133

on a combination, of the four perspectives. The behavioral therapies (see Chapter 14), for instance, concentrate on learned patterns of behavior as the source of the patient's distress. *elaborate more*

As we have said, not all people with depressed mood have an
affective disorder. Some are better understood as being troubled
(demoralized), rather than as having a disease. They usually need
more psychotherapy and little, if any, medication.

For patients who do have clinical depression, psychotherapy
(used in addition to the necessary medications or other treatments)
can sustain their hope while providing them with insight into how
illness is affecting their lives. Having a depressive illness, after
all, can cause or aggravate many other problems.

Psychotherapy requires the active and willing participation of
the patient. As a general rule, therefore, the more severe the
depression or mania, the more encouraging or directive the psychotherapist must be. In cases where mania or depression is most
severe, patients will generally not be able to participate mean-
ingfully until they improve.

Supportive Psychotherapy

Supportive psychotherapy is the most widely applicable form of
psychotherapy for those with affective disorders. It seeks to convey the realities about depression or mania to patients whose
abilities to understand their illnesses are impaired. Dr. Sidney
Bloch has emphasized that "supportive psychotherapy" means to
"carry" the patient. He has described its objectives:

1. To promote the patient's best psychological and social functioning

2. To bolster self-esteem and self-confidence

3. To make the patient aware of what can and cannot be
   achieved—his or her own limitations and the limitations of
   treatment

4. To prevent undue dependency on professional support and unnecessary hospitalizations

5. To promote the best use of available support from family and friends

Supportive psychotherapy not only is compatible with the medical treatment of depression, but also depends on the disease perspective to provide information on the patient's diagnosis, the probable cause of his or her illness, the rationale for its treatment, and, finally, its prognosis. Depressed patients who blame themselves for being depressed may be comforted by a psychiatrist who emphasizes the fact that depressive symptoms are caused by a disease. Those who have a difficult time believing that their health could ever be restored must be told that the prognosis for properly treated depression is actually very good.

A persistently delivered message is essential in supportive psychotherapy. Therapists may have to repeat their properly optimistic themes many times in order to achieve only temporary benefits in the patient's view of his or her condition and prognosis. Recovered patients often report that the persistent hopefulness of others kept them from giving up before treatment worked or before the illness remitted on its own "schedule."

Fortunately, affective illness is never hopeless. Even if the patient's particular disorder cannot be helped with current medical treatments, new treatments are always being developed. Furthermore, affective illness frequently ends in spontaneous remission (sometimes when we least expect it). The truthful message to be communicated is that success is almost always the outcome of determined treatment.

Family members need education and emotional support as well. They will play a particularly important role in the treatment of the ill person. Often, family members are the only ones able to persuade a depressed or manic patient to stay in the hospital or to accept outpatient treatments. Depressed people frequently believe that they can't be helped or don't deserve to be helped.

Some are convinced that their doctors are misguided (which is, of course, possible). Others suffer delusions and may even believe that their caretakers are demons.

The supportive psychotherapy for manic patients can be particularly difficult. Those with mania usually have a very difficult time accepting the fact that they suffer from a disease requiring immediate medical treatment, that they need supervision in spending their money or their time, and that they cannot trust their confident and cheerful feelings to lead them to rational actions. Often, supportive therapy of a manic patient takes the form of finding any area of mutual understanding that will allow a short-term agreement to be reached about his or her treatment. These agreements can "carry" the patient, his or her family and friends, and the psychiatrist until a more normal mood state returns.

Other forms of psychotherapy also have a role in treating patients with affective disorders (usually depression). A study conducted by the National Institute of Mental Health showed that, in outpatients with depressions of mild and moderate severity, at least two kinds of short-term psychotherapy—cognitive and interpersonal—were helpful. How such psychotherapy works remains (in case you put away your "What are you treating?" flag) unknown.

Whatever the mechanism, however, the success of psychotherapy in certain patient groups reinforces its value as an important part of the treatment plan for patients with depression.

Cognitive Therapy

Individuals suffering from depression often perceive themselves as having exaggerated weaknesses and dwell on how such inadequacies might prove ruinous in the future. The goal of cognitive therapy is to correct such negative thinking habits and, thereby, lessen depressed feelings. The therapist confronts the patient with the distortions in his or her self-image and view of the world. Role playing, the daily recording of negative thoughts, and the demonstration of success in assigned simple tasks at home might be used to augment discussions. As noted above, this approach can help moderately depressed patients and often is used in conjunction with medication therapy.

While many cognitive therapists believe that learned negative thinking habits are actually the cause of major depression, others believe that these habits are the result of an underlying disease process. They adapt their techniques to challenge the patient's negativism in not accepting depression as a treatable illness.

Interpersonal Therapy

Relationships are often thrown into disarray after a person becomes depressed. In other individuals, it may be that a specific failed relationship helps bring about the depression in the first place. Which came first—the depression or the problem in interpersonal relations—is an important question, but it may not be answerable.

The interpersonal therapist is concerned with the here and now. His or her goal is to reestablish normal relationships between the depressed person and others by counseling the patient and, sometimes, his or her family or friends. As social functioning improves, it is hoped, the symptom of depression will fade.

The techniques of interpersonal therapy are precisely described in a manual for therapists. Again, this type of therapy has been shown to help moderately depressed outpatients and is often used with medications.

Behavioral Therapy

A host of behavioral therapies have been espoused to break the cycle in which depressed feelings lead to abnormal behaviors that perpetuate the affective disorder. A depressed executive dismissed from his or her job, for example, might become even more despondent, reclusive, and unconfident. This could, in turn, make the next position more difficult to obtain, reinforcing the maladaptive behaviors. Behavioral therapists attempt to extinguish the patient's negative behaviors and to maximize the reinforcement of positive behaviors. Although it has not been proved that these therapies work for depressive syndromes, they are useful in helping patients overcome phobias, obsessive-compulsive symptoms, eating disorders, and other behavioral problems that complicate some depressions.

Psychoanalytic Therapy

Psychoanalytic therapy, which was developed by Sigmund Freud, seeks to unearth the unconscious conflicts that are believed to contribute to psychiatric symptoms. The theory holds that crucial experiences during childhood create inner conflicts and that the mental energy used to keep the conflicts and early life experiences unconscious creates the symptoms. Depression, for example, is sometimes understood by psychoanalysts as anger turned inward following a loss. Exposing the source of the anger is proposed as a way of dealing with it more realistically and relieving the depression in the process.

Psychodynamic therapy can last years and, in its original form (psychoanalysis), is not well suited to actively depressed or manic patients who need guidance and reassurance. The newer, shorter-term psychotherapies derived from psychoanalysis (including cognitive and interpersonal therapies) are more useful for depressed patients. Once the depression has resolved, patients can be expected to be more active in their psychotherapy and can decide whether they wish to further explore issues that were touched upon during the active treatment of the depression.

insight therapy
supportive therapy.

A Caution

We must emphasize that the use of psychotherapy alone in clinically severe depression has not shown consistent evidence of success. The techniques are clearly inappropriate for patients who are so depressed that they find it difficult to communicate; these therapies are equally ill-advised for those who are suffering with psychotic symptoms or are suicidal. Psychotherapy in which the therapist is passive, rather than supportive and actively interacting with the patient, may be misinterpreted by the patient and may worsen the sense of hopelessness and guilt.

While we do not recommend psychotherapy alone as a remedy for severe depression, supportive psychotherapy in which a caring and empathic psychiatrist guides and encourages the patient is an essential part of the treatment for depression. Patients should be seen in regularly scheduled therapy sessions. During these meetings, in addition to monitoring symptoms (especially any suicidal feelings), the therapist would discuss with the patient the nature of depression as an illness, the fact that it will improve with treatment, and the advisability of deferring major life decisions until depressive symptoms have resolved. As we have already discussed, some of the habits that come with depression and some of the consequences of unfortunate choices a person may have made when manic can live on after the illness is gone. Patients facing these difficulties often benefit from one or more of the psychotherapeutic interventions we have described.

Psychotherapy has its roots in the life story perspective, with its empathic appreciation of human suffering. When chapters in an individual's life story include affective episodes, psychotherapy can make the disease less destructive. It is this synthesis of perspectives in psychiatry that allows us to recognize depression and mania as diseases and to understand the personal nature of the suffering of affected individuals.

CHAPTER

Drug Therapy

Can'st thou not minister to a mind diseased,
Pluck from the memory a rooted sorrow,
Raze out the written troubles of the brain,
And with some sweet oblivious antidote,
Cleanse the stuffed bosom of that perilous stuff
Which weighs upon the heart?
— William Shakespeare,
Macbeth (1623)

Tricyclic Antidepressants

For patients with depression of moderate to severe intensity, tricyclic antidepressants together with psychotherapy are the treatment of choice. Approximately 70 percent of patients will experience substantial relief of depressive symptoms within four to six weeks.

Tricyclics are named for the three-ring chain in their chemical structure. The first of them, imipramine, was introduced in 1957. Its antidepressant action was discovered by Dr. Roland Kuhn, a Swiss psychiatrist who had been evaluating imipramine as a possible treatment for schizophrenia. When it failed in schizophrenics, he tried it in depressed patients, and it was remarkably successful.

All clinically effective tricyclic antidepressants have been found to have an intriguing pharmacological effect in common. After a

141

chemical message between neurons (nerve cells) has been delivered, much of the neurotransmitter is reabsorbed by the cell that released it. It is then inactivated. In this way, the "volume" of the chemical message is controlled. Tricyclic antidepressants inhibit the reabsorption and inactivation of norepinephrine and serotonin, two of the catecholamine neurotransmitters thought to be out of balance in depressed individuals. Lingering in the space around the target neuron, these chemical messengers can continue to exert their effects.

The blockade of the reuptake occurs immediately with tricyclics, raising the question of why patients do not improve for two to four weeks (and sometimes longer). The answer may be that it takes this long for the norepinephrine and serotonin molecules to cause receptor changes. Studies have shown that, after weeks, nerve cells faced with an increased level of norepinephrine and serotonin decrease the number of receptors on their surfaces. This modulation of communication between neurons may correspond to the observed change in mood.

A number of additional tricyclic antidepressants have followed imipramine (see Table 2). In any individual, one of these may seem to be more effective than another. The principal concern in choosing one, however, is to minimize side effects, which fall into three main categories: *sedative* (causing drowsiness), *hypotensive* (causing light-headedness or dizziness on standing), and *anticholinergic* (causing symptoms like dry mouth, blurred vision, constipation, and increased heart rate). Less commonly, increased appetite with weight gain, slightly slowed electrical conduction through the heart, and, rarely, blood abnormalities can also occur.

Side effects, if present, often decrease or disappear with continued treatment. Tricyclics can also frequently be given at bedtime to simplify pill-taking schedules and to reduce daytime sedation. Still, as many as a third of the patients taking tricyclics cannot tolerate the side effects and stop treatment. Psychiatrists try, therefore, to forecast which patients are more likely than others to have problems. For young people who operate heavy machinery, it would be most desirable to steer clear of sedative

Table 2. Tricyclics and Their Side Effects

TRICYCLICS		SIDE EFFECTS		
Generic Name	Trade Name	Sedative	Hypotensive	Anticholinergic
Imipramine	Tofranil SK-Pramine Presamine	Medium	More	Medium
Amitriptyline	Elavil Endep	More	More	More
Desipramine	Norpramin Pertofrane	Less	Medium	Medium
Doxepin	Sinequan Adapin	More	Medium	More
Nortriptyline	Aventyl Pamelor	Less	Medium	Medium
Protriptyline	Vivactil	Less	Medium	Medium
Trimipramine	Surmontil	More	Medium	Medium

effects. For the elderly, the lowering of blood pressure can be especially hazardous, as it may cause falls.

It is important to be aware that tricyclics can interact with other medications. The psychiatrist should be told of all other drugs the patient is taking. Likewise, the family doctor should be made aware of the antidepressant.

Treatment with tricyclics starts out slowly; dosages are gradually increased over time. For some of the drugs, maximum effectiveness and minimal side effects depend on keeping the concentrations of the medication in the blood within a fairly narrow range. Frequent blood samples may, therefore, be necessary to track the rising levels.

A fair trial of tricyclics can require eight weeks. For this reason, electroconvulsive therapy (ECT), which acts faster, is often a better choice for patients who are suicidal, who have very powerful depressive delusions (see page 40), or who have dangerous nutritional deficiencies from not eating. This is especially true in older patients who also have other medical illnesses.

Monoamine Oxidase Inhibitors

When a first-choice tricyclic antidepressant fails to relieve the symptoms of depression, either another tricyclic or a noncyclic antidepressant may be tried. One kind of noncyclic medication in the psychiatrist's armamentarium of treatment options is the monoamine oxidase inhibitor (MAOI).

Monoamine oxidase is a normal enzyme in the body whose job is to help inactivate chemical messengers spilled by neurons. It does so by removing a chemical structure called the *amine group* from neurotransmitters such as norepinephrine and serotonin. Monoamine oxidase inhibitors block the enzyme, again allowing more message volume to be sent from cell to cell in the form of transmitter molecules.

Iproniazid, the first MAOI, was originally used in the treatment of tuberculosis. Doctors administering the drug noted that a few of their patients seemed to become euphoric out of proportion to the happiness that might be expected from overcoming their disease. In 1956, the psychiatrist Nathan Kline used iproniazid in his depressed patients and noted dramatic improvement.

Since then, three descendants of iproniazid have been approved to treat depression. These are tranylcypromine (trade name, Parnate), phenelzine (Nardil) and isocarboxazide (Marplan). They are thought to be particularly useful in depressed patients with symptoms of extreme anxiety, social phobias, increased sleep, and increased appetite (all of which are common in atypical depression). They can, however, be used in any form of depressive illness.

Patients taking MAOIs experience, to a lesser extent, some of the same side effects as those taking tricyclic antidepressants.

In addition, they must restrict their diets in a prescribed manner to avoid the risk of *hypertensive crisis*, a sudden increase in blood pressure. This is due to an accumulation of an amino acid called *tyramine* that occurs naturally in some foods (cheeses and red wine, for example). Tyramine, which can cause a rise in blood pressure, is normally not a problem because it is broken down by monoamine oxidase. But with the enzyme inhibited, the amino acid can accumulate to dangerous levels. Those taking MAOIs must, therefore, abide by fairly strict dietary restrictions, as noted below.

Foods to Avoid When Taking MAOIs

Cheese, especially when aged (Cottage cheese and cream cheese need not be avoided.)
Pickled herring
Yogurt containing active bacterial cultures
Wine, especially Chianti, sherry, and red wine
Beer
Sour cream
Broad bean pods, especially Italian
Concentrated yeast preparations (Bread need not be avoided.)

Patients taking MAOIs must also avoid several prescription and over-the-counter medications, as listed below. The antianxiety agent buspirone, the antidepressant fluoxetine, decongestants, weight reduction agents, and other drugs can interact with the MAOIs to cause hypertension. The use of cyclic antidepressants with MAOIs is not recommended except under strict supervision of a physician. (Naturally, patients should read the warning labels of *all* medications to ensure safety.)

Medications to Avoid When Taking MAOIs

Demerol, a prescription pain reliever (generic name: meperidine)

Buspar, an antianxiety medication (generic name: buspirone)
Prozac, an antidepressant medication (generic name: fluoxe-
    tine)
Decongestants
Stimulants
Sympathomimetics, drugs used to raise blood pressure

Patients should be aware of the signs of a dangerous rise in blood
pressure. These include headache, stiff neck, or pounding heart-
beat. Less frequently, nausea, vomiting, and dilated pupils may
occur. Should a patient experience such symptoms, he or she
should go immediately to an emergency medical facility for possible treatment. A number of drugs, including a drug called phentolamine (Regitine) and another called nifedipine (Procardia), can
bring the blood pressure quickly back to normal.

When prescribed by experienced physicians for patients who
follow the required precautions, the MAOIs are quite safe. The
treatment has been effective for many depressed patients.

Lithium

In 1949, Dr. John Cade, an Australian psychiatrist, discovered
that lithium, a naturally occurring salt, relieved the symptoms of
mania. The first manic patient he administered the drug to was
a 51-year-old man who had been in a constant agitated state for
five years. Within a few weeks, the man's mood returned to
normal and stayed there, allowing him to return to the community
and to work.

Since its introduction, lithium (Eskalith, Lithobid, Lithotabs,
etc.) has proved to be an effective treatment for mania and depression and has become the major long-term therapy to ward off
recurrences of either mood disorder. It somehow stabilizes affectively ill patients who would otherwise tend to extremes of low
or elevated mood.

The effectiveness of lithium should raise the question: "What are you treating?" (see Chapter 16). Its all-purpose relief highlights the fact that we have much more to learn about the basic mechanisms of affective illness. If we understood better the chemical and electrical abnormalities at the root of depression and mania, we might see more clearly how a simple metal lends a very welcome helping hand.

It is essential that the level of lithium in the blood be measured regularly in those taking it. In excess, the drug can cause sluggishness and can even bring about a dangerous state of intoxication in which the patient is disoriented, tremulous, and generally ill. In a small percentage of people, lithium can also affect kidney function, making a yearly kidney-function assessment advisable.

More common side effects include mild hand tremor, temporary digestive disturbances (like nausea or diarrhea), and increased thirst and urination.

New Medications

The number of pharmacological treatments available continues to expand. While many medications are being tested for their usefulness in relieving symptoms of depression, six types are generating the most excitement. Many of these drugs have not yet been used enough in practice to have won the tried and true badge of confidence from psychiatrists. They are not, therefore, the first line of therapy.

ANTISEIZURE MEDICATIONS

Patients with epilepsy, an illness marked by recurrent seizures, are treated with anticonvulsants to block the abnormal electrical discharges in their brains. Since the 1970s, a number of studies have suggested that at least two antiseizure medications—carbamazepine (Tegretol) and valproic acid (Depakene)—decrease mood swings and related abnormal behaviors.

Like lithium, carbamazepine and, possibly, valproic acid seem to work in both depression and mania. Researchers have suggested that their effectiveness might mean that people with affective illness have underlying seizure disorders that are responsible for their symptoms. Indeed, the medications have been found to damp the electrical excitability of the limbic region of the brain, which has been implicated in the regulation of emotion.

Other experts, however, believe the antiseizure and antidepressant-antimanic effects of the medications work through different mechanisms. Carbamazepine, for example, has a structure closely resembling that of the tricyclics and interacts with many neurotransmitter systems. Scientists have taken special note of its dual ability to block the reuptake of norepinephrine and, under different circumstances, to block the neurotransmitter's release. Carbamazepine might act as a kind of neurotransmitter thermostat, forcing norepinephrine back toward normal from either underactivity or overactivity. Unlike the tricyclics, carbamazepine does not seem to work through the serotonin system.

Side effects of carbamazepine and valproic acid include sedation, gastrointestinal discomfort (diarrhea, cramps, constipation), incoordination, dizziness (with carbamazepine), and, rarely, liver or blood disorders. As with any of the medications described, these drugs should be taken with the close guidance of a physician.

The promise of antiseizure medications should again raise the question: "What are you treating?" (see Chapter 16). As we have already pointed out, psychiatry today is able to offer effective treatments for affective disorders. While this is fortunate, not knowing exactly how the medications work handicaps our ability to predict which treatment will be best for each patient.

BENZODIAZEPINES

These drugs, including Valium and Librium, have long been used in the treatment of anxiety. At least one from the family, alprazolam (Xanax), has also been recognized as having some antidepressant activity. Others of interest include clonazepam (Klonopin) and lorazepam (Ativan). These last two have possible antimanic activity.

Alprazolam, approved for treating depression by the Food and Drug Administration, has none of the tricyclic side effects, but it carries some risk of addiction and can cause a fair degree of sedation. Like the other benzodiazepines, alprazolam is probably most helpful as a bridge of relief until traditional antidepressants begin to work. The drug is also a good short-term treatment for episodes of severe anxiety called panic attacks.

It is interesting to note that clonazepam, which is useful in diffusing the anxiety that sometimes accompanies depression, is also an effective antiseizure medication.

NEUROLEPTIC AND RELATED DRUGS

Neuroleptic drugs, sometimes called *antipsychotic drugs*, are first-line drugs for schizophrenia. They are also important treatments in the initial stages of manic episodes. Many neuroleptics have only antipsychotic and antimanic features. Others, however, may have the additional effect of elevating mood in some depressed patients.

We are unable to explain why one neuroleptic is useful in alleviating depression and another is not. This is because we still lack the knowledge of exactly how these medications work at the molecular level.

One drug related to the neuroleptics is called amoxapine (Ascendin). Amoxapine has been shown to be as effective as tricyclic antidepressants in relieving depression. While it compares quite favorably with tricyclics in terms of sedative, hypotensive, and anticholinergic side effects, however, it shares with neuroleptics the risk of movement disorders. The worst of these is called *tardive dyskinesia*, a condition that causes uncontrollable and sometimes debilitating movements (particularly of the face and neck) that can be permanent.

OTHER CYCLIC ANTIDEPRESSANTS

The chain-link structure is common to a host of other medications currently being evaluated for their effectiveness in treating depression. One of these is maprotiline (Ludiomil). Maprotiline is a four-ring chemical that is as effective as the tricyclics in treating depression, but it is less likely to cause sedation or anticholinergic side effects.

SEROTONIN REUPTAKE INHIBITORS

We have already described the ability of tricyclics to inhibit the reabsorption and inactivation of norepinephrine and serotonin. Serotonin reuptake inhibitors preferentially or exclusively block the reuptake of serotonin alone.

Two such medications are fluoxetine (Prozac) and trazadone (Desyrel). These have fewer anticholinergic side effects and relieve depression as well as do the tricyclics. Trazadone, which has been studied for longer than fluoxetine, has the disadvantage of being quite sedating. Fluoxetine is less sedating, but it may take a bit longer before beginning to work.

STIMULANTS

It makes some intuitive sense that people suffering from depression, characterized as it is by decreased energy, might respond to stimulant medications. Two of these, methylphenidate

(Ritalin) and dextroamphetamine (Dexedrine), have been used with some success in treatment. It is not clear, however, that stimulants work as well as more standard medications (e.g., tricyclics) or that they work when the mainstay medications have failed. They also carry a significant risk of dependence, among other side effects.

For these reasons, stimulant therapy for depression is close to being a last-resort treatment. In the small number of cases in which it works dramatically well, however, it is a valuable ally.

Combination Drug Therapy

Sometimes two or even three medications used together seem to work better than any one alone. For this reason, when a single medication fails to relieve the symptoms of depression or manic-depressive illness, combinations of medications may be tried. These include tricyclic-lithium, tricyclic-methylphenidate, and MAOI-lithium partnerships. As we already mentioned, a neuroleptic (antipsychotic) is sometimes used with a tricyclic in patients with prominent delusions as part of their depressive symptoms. Antianxiety drugs may also play a role in multidrug regimens, especially in the early phases of treatment, before the antidepressant goes to work.

A few combination drugs intermix two different medications into one pill, as follows:

Etrafon = Triavil = amitriptyline (a tricyclic) + perphenazine (an antipsychotic)

Limbitrol = amitriptyline + chlordiazepoxide (an antianxiety agent)

Whether a psychiatrist uses these combination drugs may depend on whether he or she is comfortable with the proportion of ingredients or would rather have more control over the dosage of each.

A number of novel combinations also hold some promise for

stubborn depressions. Adding synthetic thyroid hormone to a tricyclic antidepressant may speed relief in some cases—even when the patient's thyroid is normal. L-tryptophan, the major building block of the neurotransmitter serotonin, can be used to boost the effects of other antidepressants.

The simultaneous use of a number of medications to treat depression requires that the psychiatrist pay strict attention to drug interactions and side effects. No patient should hazard a combination of his or her own.

CHAPTER

Other Therapies

It may help someone else to know that with my type of illness, though you may not believe it during your illness, there is an end to the dark tunnel in which you wander lost and alone for so long. There is an end, and an opening with a light to guide you back to the world you thought you had lost forever.
— Barbara Benziger,
The Prison of My Mind (1968)

ECT

Electroconvulsive therapy (ECT) provides the most rapid relief of any treatment for severe depression. Partly because of the anesthesia required and partly because of the stigma still associated with the treatment, it is usually given only to hospitalized patients. It should be considered when drug therapy has failed, when the patient is at high risk for suicide or starvation, or when depression is judged to be overwhelmingly severe. It is also particularly useful when the depressed person is troubled by delusions or hallucinations.

The long and complex history of ECT began fifty years ago when Ugo Cerletti and Lucio Bini, two Italian psychiatrists, proposed it as a treatment for many forms of mental illness. While the new therapy was extremely effective in relieving severe depression, it rapidly acquired a bad reputation. Some hospitals used it indiscriminately, believing it would do no harm and knowing that it could induce miraculous recoveries. Without the anesthesia now available to psychiatrists, it frightened patients and sometimes caused uncontrolled seizures.

Today's ECT is quite different. Electric current is still applied to the patient's head (for about two seconds), but the amount of electricity used is far less than in the past. The patient is also given anesthetic agents to ensure that he or she is asleep, with completely relaxed muscles. This kind of anesthesia means that the electrical seizure activity in the brain (which lasts thirty to sixty seconds) does not translate to seizure activity in the body. The entire procedure takes about twenty minutes and is usually repeated six to twelve times, over several weeks, until a remission occurs. In one study, 49 percent of patients who had received ECT treatments rated a trip to the dentist as more upsetting.

How ECT works is a mystery. We know that the electricity passing through the brain must induce electrical seizure activity to be effective. We have also learned that ECT alters the receptors for the catecholamine neurotransmitters in a way similar to that of the tricyclic antidepressants. Still, we fail to understand just why depression lifts, and once again must ask, "What are you treating?" (see Chapter 16).

The major side effect of ECT is memory loss. Forty percent of patients report spotty loss of new and old memories for weeks to months after treatment. They may have difficulty recalling the names of recent acquaintances, such as a doctor or a nurse. After a month, the memory loss is generally no longer apparent to friends and family. Sensitive testing has revealed minor defects after three months, but these resolve within six months.

Despite the reassuring results of extensive research with memory testing, some patients complain of persisting problems. Usually, the memory loss they report is for events that occurred around the time of treatment rather than for new (or more distant) memories. This pattern is called a *retrograde amnesia* and is not to be confused with new learning, the most vital aspect of memory.

It is important to remember that recurrent depression can also impair memory.

Other side effects include headache, muscle ache, nausea, and the infrequent, but sometimes serious, problems associated with anesthesia.

Phototherapy and Sleep Therapies

Doctors since Hippocrates (400 B.C.) have noted that some people seem to suffer from depressive episodes that come and go with the change of seasons. As we mentioned in Chapter 8, the pattern of such seasonal affective disorders (most commonly winter depressions and spring hypomanias) may be related to differences in the amount of sunlight people are exposed to.

In order to test the hypothesis, researchers at the National Institute of Mental Health and at other centers began treating people suffering from seasonal depression with exposure to bright light for several hours a day. Their results showed that the treatment helped most depressed people within the first week and that stopping treatment resulted in a similarly rapid relapse.

How bright-light therapy helps is still unclear. One theory is that it works by modulating the amount of certain neurotransmitters in the brain. Interestingly enough, serotonin levels vary with the seasons, being lowest during fall and winter.

If artificially altering the body's interpretation of the seasons wards off depression, what about altering other cycles, such as the sleep-wake cycle?

Sleep deprivation (restriction of sleep), in fact, has also been shown to bring rapid but very transient improvement in symptoms of depression. Different strategies have been employed, including total sleep deprivation for twenty-four hours, restriction of sleep to the second half of the night, and curtailment of the part of sleep called the rapid-eye-movement (REM) phase, the period during which dreaming occurs.

We do not know how alterations in sleep patterns blunt the symptoms of depression. We are reminded again, therefore, of the gap between our knowledge of what works and exactly why it works: What basic brain mechanisms are our very successful therapies able to restore?

CHAPTER

Future Therapies:
The Hope and the Promise

*What can we expect from this path? We can expect the
results that Osler promised and delivered to medicine
itself: an understanding of the differences among the
patients we see and eventually an appreciation of the
varieties of etiology and mechanism found in different
psychiatric disorders. We can expect to realize preven-
tive strategies and effective therapies based on this
knowledge. But fundamentally, we can anticipate the
emergence of a psychiatry identified by its subject matter, unified in its conceptual base, and no longer sub-
divided into camps with different "orientations."*
                                   —Paul R. McHugh, M.D.

If a general medical doctor treating a sore throat were asked,
"What are you treating with that penicillin?" he could answer,
"Strep throat." He could grow the infecting bacterium in the
laboratory, see it destroyed by the antibiotic in culture, and know
exactly how penicillin works—by interfering with the molecular
bridging that allows bacteria to build their cell walls. Psychiatrists
treating affective disorders have much more trouble when asked,
"What are you treating?" As we have said before, this is because
psychiatrists still do not know the specific mechanisms of the

illness being treated and cannot, therefore, explain exactly how the effective therapies interfere to restore health.

But psychiatry is on its way. It is moving from what are called empirical therapies toward rational therapies, which are aimed directly and knowingly at the biochemical pathways leading to diseases.

Empirical Treatments

Empirical treatments are those that relieve distressing symptoms but work by uncertain mechanisms. In general medicine this is true for many powerful and important drugs, including aspirin and steroids. In most ground-breaking therapies, in fact, doctors first learn that the drug works and only later do they discover why it works.

During the late nineteenth century most medications prescribed not only were mysterious in mechanism of action but also were not thoroughly studied for effectiveness. This allowed quack treatments to claim remarkable therapeutic results with no true evidence of success. The public health movement was fueled, in part, by distrust and disenchantment with such spurious medications and led to a general discrediting and discarding of most drugs listed in medical manuals. They were, in a manner of speaking, dumped into the ocean, leading to the famous comment of Justice Oliver Wendell Holmes, "So much better for man and so much worse for the fish."

Separating quack treatments (that don't work) from empirical treatments (that do, but we don't know why) became easier with the development of what is called the *controlled clinical trial*. In controlled clinical trials half the patients with a given condition are treated with the drug being studied, and half are given inactive look-alike pills, called *placebos*. Who receives the real drug and who receives the placebo is random, and neither the doctor nor the patient knows whether the pill being taken really contains the drug. In this way, the results are not influenced by anyone "thinking" the medication should work. When the drug is given in a reasonable dosage for a lengthy enough period of time, the patients actually receiving it should improve more than those receiving placebos if the drug is effective.

Today, treatments for psychiatric illness should pass the controlled clinical trial test. Only through these extensive studies have we learned for sure that treatments for depression—medications, ECT, psychotherapy, and others—are both effective and reasonably safe. They do indeed work, even if we still don't know why.

Empathic Treatments

Empathic treatments are those directly aimed at the suffering of the ill person. Although all treatments are motivated by the desire to end suffering, not all focus on the suffering itself. Insulin therapy for diabetes, for instance, would not qualify, because its aim is to interrupt the disease mechanism; it does not address what the experience of illness is like for the afflicted person.

Psychotherapies, on the other hand, are good examples of empathic treatment. Although some psychiatrists would argue that psychotherapy can alter bodily function and, thus, possibly cure disease, the most traditional goal of psychotherapy is the sharing of the experience of suffering between patient and therapist. This "work" usually proceeds on two fronts. First, the psychotherapist coauthors with the patient a life story that relates the events in the patient's life to each other in a way that makes sense. Second, the therapist promotes a confiding therapist-patient relationship based on positive expectations. The desired outcome is that the patient will have an enhanced appreciation of his or her freedom to choose new directions and accept their consequences.

While empathic therapies will always play a role in relieving suffering, they, too, can be put to the empirical test: the controlled clinical trial. Psychotherapies can be objectively studied to evaluate how well they alleviate symptoms of depression or discouragement. In this way, their usefulness in helping patients understand life situations in human terms and build options for the future can be appreciated apart from their ability to reduce symptoms.

Insisting that treatments aimed at the symptoms of psychiatric illness pass the empirical test ensures that ineffective treatments will be short-lived. But psychiatry has an even brighter, rational, future.

Rational Treatments

Rational treatments for a disease actually interfere with a known disease mechanism. Examples include killing (with penicillin) the streptococcus bacteria causing strep throat and injecting patients with insulin to lower the blood-sugar level in diabetes. We envision a day when treatment and prevention of depression and manic-depressive illness will be similarly targeted to block a specific step in the mechanism of illness. Although we are not there yet, we are well on our way.

The building blocks are in place. We know we can, for example, prevent the depression caused by the antihypertensive reserpine by substituting another medication. Similarly, we know that we can prevent some of the depressions caused by stroke by timely treatment of the high blood pressure and other conditions (including diabetes) that predispose to stroke. We already know a good deal about how our medications interact with neurotransmitter systems. Furthermore, we are starting to learn about hormonal therapies, light therapies, and sleep-related therapies.

Completely new treatments may emerge from molecular genetic research. We can imagine, for example, identifying a disease-causing gene coding for affective illness and finding out that the protein it makes is either deficient in amount or abnormal in structure. A normal protein might then be synthesized and administered to correct the pathology and block, once and for all, the symptoms of depression and mania. Other fertile molecular research is exploring the role of cell membranes, receptors, and intracellular (within one cell rather than between cells) chemical messengers.

All these treatments will have to be proved in controlled clinical trials. But insisting that they pass both the empirical and rational tests means exploring *how* they work. We know from past experience that rational explanations for a treatment's success open the door to deeper questions and further discovery. Insulin therapy for diabetes, after all, is a rational treatment. It addresses directly the body's inability to produce the hormone. However, the fact that it prevents high blood-sugar levels without necessarily reversing or preventing many long-term complications of the illness shows us how much more we have to learn.

The process of developing rational treatments for affective illnesses will surely be one that similarly depends on new understandings raising new questions leading to new research. The cement that will make the foundation of discovery secure is the commitment to use each of the perspectives of psychiatry in its place and to its fullest potential.

Out of the Dark and into the Light

As psychiatry moves toward rational treatments for illnesses that are now mysterious in mechanism, the disease, personality, behavior, and life story perspectives will all be powerful tools. This is because each one helps people with affective illness to live healthier and more productive lives.

We have said that we believe the most illuminating way to view depression and manic-depressive illness is as diseases. But using the disease perspective to understand and treat depression or manic-depressive illness in no way disenfranchises a psychiatrist from the other three perspectives. Rather, it compels him or her to explore how personality traits, behaviors, and life story events might be coloring the patient's illness and contributing to the patient's suffering. In other words, the psychiatrist's calling is not to join the "brain doctor camp" or the "mind doctor camp" but to understand and put to use the best ideas from each in the treatment of patients.

An Invitation

While writing this book, we recalled the many painful but inspiring experiences of our patients. Those we have treated have helped us understand what it means to suffer from affective illness. Sustaining their courage and the strength of their families in the face of adversity is a central motivation behind this book.

If you, a family member, or a friend has a story to tell about depression or manic-depressive illness, please feel free to write to us about your experiences. We would feel privileged to share your thoughts, if only by mail. Write us at Diseases of Mood, c/o Keith Ablow, M.D., P.O. Box 541, Marblehead, MA 01945.

Frequently Asked Questions about Depression and Manic-Depressive Illness

1. *How do I find a doctor?*

First, tell your family physician about the way you have been feeling. Your own doctor has the most knowledge about your medical history, and many internists and family practitioners also have experience in treating depression. If you are already seeing a nonphysician psychotherapist, tell him or her about your symptoms and your concern that you may have a depressive disorder that also needs medical treatment.

In cases in which you, your doctor, or your therapist feels that the symptoms of depression are severe or that a first-choice treatment is not working, referral to a psychiatrist is the appropriate strategy. Your family physician or therapist may be best able to suggest an expert in your community. Otherwise, a close friend or family member may have personal knowledge of a professional who can evaluate and treat you.

Sometimes it may seem that no one is directing you to a physician whose special interest and expertise is in affective illness. You should feel free to call your local medical or psychiatric society and ask for a referral. You might also contact one of several very helpful mental health organizations (see pages 171 to 174). Finally, another direct route to treatment is to call a university hospital in your area and ask to speak with the outpatient psychiatry office or, if one is available, the director of a depression or affective disorders clinic.

2. What should I do if the doctor's diagnosis seems mysterious or I don't understand the suggested treatment plan for my condition?

Your first appointment with a primary-care physician or a psychiatrist will ordinarily start with a session in which you give your history and answer the doctor's questions. It should conclude with an open discussion about what condition might be causing your symptoms and an outline of a preliminary treatment plan. Feel free to ask questions and to relate honestly to your doctor the extent of your suffering. Even at times when it is difficult, you will need to participate actively in the evaluation of your condition so that you will understand the treatment plan.

3. How can I help a friend or family member with depression?

Psychiatric illness unfortunately still carries with it a social stigma. Many individuals who would benefit from treatment believe that seeking help is a sign of weakness or a source of shame. They need much support from family and friends who convincingly state that starting on the road to health by getting treatment is a sign of strength, not a token of disgrace.

Because depression and mania are often accompanied by symptoms of indecision or poor judgment, which makes planning quite difficult, a friend or family member may need to help initiate or follow through with plans for an evaluation and, then, with treatment. "Making sure" a depressed or manic patient complies with prescribed medications and scheduled appointments can help speed recovery but can also cause conflicts if the ill person feels discounted in the process. If possible, a family member should "negotiate" with the ill person about which types of encouragement are welcome.

As we talked about in Chapter 13, it is important to strive to understand, without becoming alarmed, the normal emotions a recovering individual may express. It is also important, however, to be sensitive to clear signs of continued or increased illness, especially any suggestion that the person is contemplating suicide. In such cases, the issue should be discussed directly with the individual and, if needed, with both the individual and his or her physician.

4. Should I stop my medication as soon as I think the depression has lifted?

Absolutely not. Antidepressants may relieve the symptoms of depression while the illness runs its course over months or years. Stopping medication prematurely could cause a relapse; discontinuing it should be done only with the close guidance of your physician.

5. Do I need to stay on medication for life?

The need for lithium and/or antidepressant medication is specific to a person's illness. For people who experience severe or frequent exacerbations of major affective disorders, medications may always be needed. For those who experience long, symptom-free time periods in between recurrences, medications may be needed only intermittently.

It is important for anyone with a major affective disorder to maintain close contact with a psychiatrist, who will monitor his or her moods and decide on appropriate therapy.

6. Why do I need to have blood drawn while I am on an antidepressant or lithium?

Blood sampling allows your physician to monitor the blood concentrations of medications you are taking. In very high concentration, lithium and other antidepressant and antimanic medications can be dangerous. In addition to guarding against toxicity, blood testing allows for optimal dosing of medications with a "therapeutic window." These medications work best within a specific range of concentrations, above which and below which they are less effective.

7. Can I become addicted to antidepressants?

Antidepressant medications and lithium are not addictive. People do not develop cravings for them. Some antidepressants should, however, be tapered, rather than stopped abruptly, when no longer needed. This allows the body to adjust to their absence.

8. What is postpartum depression?

Postpartum depression refers to depression occurring after childbirth. While some women experience severe major depression following childbirth, many others experience only transient mood changes (apparently due to the hormonal changes). Many of those who suffer more severely have experienced a major affective illness before pregnancy or will experience one at some point (possibly unrelated to childbirth) later in life. The treatment of the persistent severe depressive episodes following childbirth is no different from that for episodes occurring at other times. The biggest problem related to these disorders is delayed recognition and treatment, which affects not only the depressed mother, but her infant and the rest of her family.

9. Does affective illness occur in children and adolescents?

It is clear that children and adolescents have substantial rates of serious depression and manic-depressive illness. These conditions are painful and can result in social, familial, and educational problems. They also carry the risk of suicide.

There has been a worrisome increase in suicides among adolescents and young adults in recent years. The reasons for this are not known, but it may be related to increased use and abuse of alcohol and other drugs. This, in turn, may be related to affective illness.

It is important that the signs and symptoms of affective illness in children and adolescents be identified by parents and taken seriously. Loss of appetite, fatigue, lethargy, unusual irritability or sadness (possibly reflected only in facial expression), and new difficulties in school may be clues.

When depression or manic-depressive illness is suspected, parents should seek the help of their family physician or, if possible, a psychiatrist experienced in diagnosing and treating affective disorders.

10. *Are the elderly especially prone to depression?*

Depression in our growing elderly community can be extremely severe and is fairly common. Symptoms such as decreased mood, decreased self-esteem, loss of interest in pleasurable activities, and loss of appetite are not "normal" parts of aging. The likelihood of concurrent medical conditions that can cause or complicate depression makes medical diagnosis and treatment of affective illness in the elderly essential. About a third of depressed patients over the age of 60 experience memory and other intellectual impairments that will improve when the depression is successfully treated.

11. *Can a poor diet cause depression?*

Although appetite often wanes during depression, there is no evidence that eating the wrong foods will cause major affective illness. Alcohol, of course, can play a role in making depression much worse.

12. *Can vitamins relieve depression?*

While the amino acid L-tryptophan may be of some usefulness in helping to treat some depressions, it is probably not effective alone. Therefore, it is usually used (if at all) with standard anti-depressants or lithium. Uncommonly, vitamin deficiencies can be associated with depression, but there is no good evidence that they cause it. There is no evidence that vitamins, minerals, or nutritional supplements alone are useful in the treatment of major depression.

13. *Is there any difference between generic and trade brands of a drug?*

While the same chemical is found in generic and trade brands of a particular drug, the pills (even when the same size and weight) may differ in *bioavailability*—the amount of the drug that is free to enter the circulation and reach the brain. For this reason, it is sometimes wise to continue with a single brand throughout a treatment course. This decision should be made by your doctor or your doctor and pharmacist together.

Organizations That Provide Help

You can learn more and you can help. Several organizations that have current programs to educate the public and encourage further research into affective disorders are discussed below.

The Depression/Awareness, Recognition, and Treatment (D/ART) Program is a national public education campaign on depressive illnesses that was launched in 1988 by the National Institute of Mental Health (NIMH), a component of the Alcohol, Drug Abuse, and Mental Health Administration. The D/ART program includes disseminating information about the symptoms and treatments of depressive illnesses. Its slogan is "Depression. Define it. Defeat it." For more information, write to D/ART, NIMH, Room 15-C-05, 5600 Fishers Lane, Rockville, MD 20857.

The Depression and Related Affective Disorders Association (DRADA) is a nonprofit organization that focuses on manic-depressive illness and depression. DRADA distributes informational materials, conducts educational meetings, and runs Young People's Outreach programs for high school counselors and nurses. The association helps individuals organize affective disorder sup-

171

port groups, and it provides leadership training programs and consultation for those groups. DRADA helps support research on the causes and treatment of depressive and manic-depressive disorders; it cosponsors, with The Johns Hopkins School of Medicine Department of Psychiatry, an annual research-education symposium for both professionals and interested laypersons. Organizationally, DRADA unites the efforts of individuals with affective disorders, family members, and mental health professionals. The association serves members in many states. For more information, write to DRADA, Meyer 4-181, Johns Hopkins, 600 N. Wolfe Street, Baltimore, MD 21205, or call (301) 955-4647.

The Manic-Depressive Illness Foundation was established to increase public awareness and understanding of the nature and treatment of manic-depressive and depressive illnesses through the use of the arts. Two "Moods and Music" concerts have been enthusiastically received and more are being planned in major cities across the United States. The group believes that public acceptance of severe mood disorders will be increased by emphasizing the links between mood disorders and creativity, initiative, energy, and leadership. For more information, write to Dr. Kay R. Jamison, President, The Manic-Depressive Illness Foundation, 2723 P Street, N.W., Washington, D.C. 20007.

The National Alliance for the Mentally Ill (NAMI) is America's largest self-help support and advocacy organization for families of persons with serious mental illnesses and for those with the illnesses themselves. Through support, education, advocacy, and research, NAMI reaches thousands of people across the country. Begun in 1979 with fewer than 300 family members, the alliance has grown to include nearly 900 affiliated support groups and 70,000 families. For more information, write to NAMI, 2101 Wilson Boulevard, Suite 302, Arlington, VA 22201, or call (703) 524-7600.

The National Alliance for Research on Schizophrenia and Depression (NARSAD) is committed to ending mental illness through research. Consisting of private citizens, psychiatrists, and scientists, NARSAD raises funds to find the causes, treatments, cures, and preventions of severe mental illnesses, primarily the schizophrenias and depressions. Areas of research to be funded are determined by a scientific council, and grants are allocated to scientists throughout North America. Localized fund-raising efforts are being organized thoroughout the country. For more information, write to NARSAD, P.O. Box 1943, Chicago, IL 60690–1943, or call (312) 641-1666.

The National Depressive and Manic-Depressive Association (NDMDA) is a patient- and family-based organization of more than 120 groups throughout the United States and Canada. NDMDA, representing well over 25,000 patient and family members, views the affective disorders as biochemical in nature, best treated with medication and adjunctive psychotherapy. The initial NDMDA support group started in 1978 in Chicago, which is now the national headquarters for the organization, and the national group—the NDMDA—was formed in 1986. The association's purpose is to provide personal support and direct services to individuals and family members suffering from clinical depression or manic-depressive illness, to educate the public concerning the nature and management of these treatable medical disorders, and to promote related research. For more information, write to NDMDA, Merchandise Mart, Box 3395, Chicago, IL 60654, or call (312) 939-2442.

The National Foundation for Depressive Illness, established in 1983 by a group of the country's leading psychopharmacologists and laypeople, provides public and professional information about affective disorders and the availability of diagnosis and treatment. The foundation's public awareness program addresses this pervasive, costly, and hidden national health issue to help eliminate the stigma often attached to those who seek psychiatric assistance. For more information, write to Roberta Maggenti, Director of Communications, The National Foundation for Depressive Illness, P.O. Box 2257, New York, NY 10016, or call (212) 620-7637 or (800) 248-4344.

The National Mental Health Association (NMHA), founded in 1909, is committed to promoting mental health, preventing mental illnesses, and improving the care and treatment of people with mental illnesses. As the nation's only citizens' volunteer group concerned with all aspects of mental health and mental illnesses, NMHA has chartered organizations in 43 states with 600 local affiliates. This voluntary network supports and participates in nationwide programs of advocacy, education, information, and volunteer services. The association also serves the public interest as the public-policy voice for mental health issues in Congress and in state legislatures. Current NMHA projects include publicizing the plight of emotionally disturbed children, reporting on the mental health of rural Americans, and coordinating a national coalition to address the needs of homeless people with mental illnesses. The NMHA information center answers hundreds of calls and letters weekly and serves as a major source of high-quality, educational mental health information for the general public. For more information, write to Gina White, The National Mental Health Association, 1021 Prince Street, Alexandria, VA 22314, or call (703) 684-7722.

Glossary

acetylcholine: The main neurotransmitter involved in muscle activity and one of the principal neurotransmitters involved in bodily functions that are automatic (such as sweating). Antidepressant medications that interfere with acetylcholine cause symptoms such as dry mouth, blurred vision, constipation, and increased heart rate.

Adapin: A trade name for the generic tricyclic antidepressant doxepin.

affective: Refers to mental experiences that include moods, emotions, and motivations. Affective experiences are often distinguished from cognitive abilities such as intelligence, memory, and reasoning.

affective disorders: Narrowly, the syndromes of depression, mania, or mixed states; more broadly, also includes anxiety states, such as panic disorder.

alprazolam: A high-potency benzodiaxepine antianxiety drug that also has antidepressant activity. Its trade name is Xanax.

amitriptyline: A tricyclic antidepressant. Trade names include Elavil and Endep.

amoxapine: An antidepressant that also has antipsychotic effects. Its trade name is Ascendin.

anorexia nervosa: A prolonged refusal to eat motivated by an abnormal fear of becoming obese. Eating disorders are frequently associated with atypical depression.

anticholinergic: Interfering with the action of the neurotransmitter acetylcholine. Anticholinergic drugs cause side effects such as dry mouth, blurred vision, constipation, and increased heart rate.

antipsychotic: A medication that helps to relieve symptoms such as delusions or hallucinations, sometimes referred to as psychotic symptoms.

anxiety disorders: Disorders in which debilitating anxiety is a central feature. The anxiety comes on as sudden panic attacks or is the result of a phobia, an obsession, or a compulsion. Anxiety symptoms are frequently associated with depression.

Ascendin: The trade name for amoxapine, an antidepressant medication that also has antipsychotic effects.

Ativan: The trade name for lorazepam, a benzodiazepine antianxiety medication.

atypical depression: A moderately severe form of affective illness that combines long periods of depression with short intervals of relief. Sleep and appetite are often increased. The onset of atypical depression may seem closely tied to distressing life events. Its victims frequently come to suffer from prominent anxiety symptoms and abnormal behaviors (e.g., eating disorders).

Aventyl: A trade name for the tricyclic antidepressant nortriptyline.

basal ganglia: Structures deep in the brain that are involved in muscle tone, movement, cognition, and affective responses.

behavioral therapy: Psychotherapy that attempts to extinguish abnormal behaviors by changing the consequences of those behaviors.

benzodiazepine: A family of antianxiety agents that includes Valium and Librium. At least one high-potency benzodiazepine, Xanax, has also shown antidepressant activity.

bipolar disorder: Affective illness in which episodes of depression keep company with episodes of mania. Persons who have experienced only manic episodes are also referred to as bipolar.

bipolar II disorder: An affective disorder in which persistent depression is intermittently interrupted by brief periods of normal or mildly hypomanic mood.

bright-light therapy: Also called *phototherapy*, a treatment for depression in which the patient is exposed to bright lights for several hours each day. The therapy was inspired by seasonally depressed individuals, some of whom experience depression during winter months when sunlight is less plentiful.

bulimia: An excessive appetite for food accompanied by an insistence on remaining thin. The conflicting goals lead to abnormal behaviors, such as binge eating and then purging (making oneself vomit). Eating disorders are frequently associated with atypical depression.

carbamazepine: An antiseizure medication that is also useful in the treatment of both mania and depression. One trade name is Tegretol.

catecholamines: A group of structurally related neurotransmitters, including dopamine, norepinephrine, and serotonin, thought to be involved in the pathology of affective disorders.

chlordiazepoxide hypochloride: A benzodiazepine antianxiety agent with the trade name Librium.

chromosome: DNA strands (made up of building blocks called genes) that determine hereditary characteristics such as hair and eye color. Each cell in the body contains 46 chromosomes organized into 23 pairs. Chromosomes 6, 11 and X (the sex chromosome) may carry genes that code for bipolar affective disorder in some individuals with the illness.

clonazepam: A benzodiazepine antianxiety agent with the trade name Klonopin. Clonazepam is also an effective antiseizure medication.

cognitive therapy: Psychotherapy for depression designed to confront and correct what is seen as an inappropriately dismal self-image and view of the world. Through techniques including discussion, role playing, and the demonstration of success in assigned simple tasks at home, the therapist attempts to expose the distortions in the patient's negative mind-set.

compulsion: A behavior that an individual feels an irresistible need to repeat again and again despite his or her better judgment or will. The behavior is designed to avoid something in the future, but it is not realistically connected with that goal or is clearly excessive. Examples include tracing a tortuously exact path of footsteps on one's way to work in order to avoid being fired or washing one's hands again and again until raw to avoid contamination by germs.

cortisol: A hormone produced by the body's adrenal glands, located above the kidneys. The secretion of cortisol by the adrenal glands is regulated by hormonal signals from the pituitary gland in the brain.

Cushing's disease: A disease in which the adrenal glands are overstimulated and, therefore, produce an overabundance of the hormone cortisol. Symptoms of mania or depression often accompany the round, moonlike facial appearance, unusual distribution of fat, diabetes, and high blood pressure usually seen in this condition.

cyclothymic disorder: Sometimes referred to as *cyclothymic personality*, a very mild affective disorder in which a person's mood swings from mildly elevated to mildly low and then back. The symptoms are not severe enough to satisfy the criteria for bipolar disorder.

delusion: A false, unshakable belief held by a person despite overwhelming evidence to the contrary. The false belief is not a widely shared one among those in the individual's religious or cultural group. A person may become convinced, for example, that he or she is dying of cancer despite a battery of tests showing that the person is completely well.

deoxyribonucleic acid: See *DNA.*

Depakene: The trade name for valproic acid, an antiseizure medication that may also be useful in treating symptoms of both depression and mania.

desipramine: A tricyclic antidepressant. Trade names include Norpramin and Pertofrane.

Desyrel: The trade name for trazadone, an antidepressant thought to work by blocking the reuptake of the neurotransmitter serotonin into the neurons that have released it.

dexamethasone: A synthetic version of the hormone cortisol. In the dexamethasone suppression test (DST), dexamethasone is given to a patient to measure whether the expected inhibition of cortisol production occurs. Patients with major depression are more likely than others to show no significant decrease in production.

Dexedrine: The trade name for dextroamphetamine, a stimulant drug that sometimes plays a role in treating depression in which other medications have failed.

dextroamphetamine: A stimulant drug that sometimes plays a role in treating depression in which other medications have failed. Its trade name is Dexedrine.

diazepam: A benzodiazepine antianxiety medication. Trade names include Valium, Valrelease, and Valcaps.

DNA (deoxyribonucleic acid): The genetic raw material of genes and chromosomes that is passed from generation to generation and determines hereditary characteristics.

dopamine: One of the catecholamine neurotransmitters. Dopamine is thought to play a role in the pathologies of schizophrenia and affective illness.

doxepin: A tricyclic antidepressant. Trade names include Sinequan and Adapin.

drive: A term that implies intrinsic biological forces that motivate behavior. Hunger, for example, may be said to drive eating behavior.

DST: See *dexamethasone*.

dysphoric mania: A mixed affective disorder combining the high energy levels, racing thoughts, and pressured speech of mania with a fearful or sad, rather than elated, mood.

dysthymic disorder: A chronic (at least two years) depressive condition that is not of sufficient severity to meet the criteria for major depression. This kind of depression may represent chronic unhappiness (not a disease) or an atypical depressive illness.

ECT (electroconvulsive therapy): The application of electric current to one or both sides of the scalp as a treatment for severe depression (or mania).

Elavil: A trade name for the tricyclic antidepressant amitriptyline.

electroconvulsive therapy: See *ECT*.

Endep: A trade name for the generic tricyclic antidepressant amitriptyline.

endocrine: Pertaining to the body's network of glands or the hormones they produce.

epidemiology: The study of the occurrence and distribution of diseases in the community.

Eskalith: A trade name for the antimanic drug lithium.

Esquirol, Jean: French psychiatrist (1772–1840); wrote the first modern textbook of psychiatry and first recognized the seasonal pattern of some affective disorders.

etiology: The most basic cause of a disease. The etiology of diabetes, for example, is thought by some to be a virus that causes injury to the pancreas.

Etrafon: A combination drug intermixing the tricyclic amitriptyline with the antipsychotic perphenazine.

fluoxetine: An antidepressant thought to work by blocking the reuptake of the neurotransmitter serotonin into the neurons that have released it. Its trade name is Prozac.

Freud, Sigmund: Austrian neurologist (1856–1939) and the "father of psychoanalysis."

Galen: Greek physician (129–199 A.D.) who practiced in Rome; a medical teacher, medical writer, and the physician to Marcus Aurelius.

genes: Considered to be the basic units of heredity. Made up of DNA, they are the building blocks of chromosomes.

hallucination: A perception without a stimulus. Hallucinations may be visual (seeing something that isn't there), auditory (hearing something that isn't there), olfactory (smelling . . .), gustatory (tasting . . .) or tactile (feeling . . .).

5-HIAA (5-hydroxyindoleacetic acid): A breakdown product formed when the neurotransmitter serotonin is metabolized.

Hippocrates: Greek physician (c. 460–c. 377 B.C.); considered the "Father of Medicine."

histamine: A widespread chemical in the body that probably also functions as a neurotransmitter in the brain. Histamine has been implicated in the pathology of affective illness.

Huntington's disease: An inherited illness that appears in midlife and usually progresses to a fatal outcome within fifteen years. Affected individuals lose their intellectual abilities and become unable to control their movements. Symptoms of manic-depressive illness often appear early in the course of Huntington's disease.

hypotension: Low blood pressure. When the low blood pressure occurs on standing it is referred to as *orthostatic hypotension*.

imipramine: A tricyclic antidepressant. Trade names include Tofranil, SK-Pramine, and Presamine.

insomnia: Inability to sleep.

interpersonal therapy: Psychotherapy that seeks to treat depression by reestablishing normal relationships between the patient and his or her family and friends.

iproniazid: The first monoamine oxidase inhibitor used to treat depression (1956). Iproniazid was originally used in the treatment of tuberculosis.

isocarboxazide: A monoamine oxidase inhibitor. Its trade name is Marplan.

Kline, Nathan: The psychiatrist who, in 1956, discovered that the antituberculosis drug iproniazid was useful in the treatment of depression.

Klonopin: The trade name of the high-potency benzodiazepine antianxiety and antimanic agent clonazepam. Klonopin is also an effective antiseizure medication.

L-dopa: A chemical from which the neurotransmitter dopamine is made. L-Dopa is used to treat Parkinson's disease.

learned helplessness: The passive acceptance of painful stimuli after a period during which escape from pain has been blocked. Learned helplessness has been proposed as an explanation for depression.

lethargy: Sluggishness or drowsiness.

Librium: The trade name for chlordiazepoxide hypochloride, a benzodiazepine antianxiety medication.

Limbitrol: A combination medication intermixing the tricyclic antidepressant amitriptyline and the antipsychotic perphenazine.

lithium: The naturally occurring mineral that is used to treat mania. Trade names include Eskalith, Lithobid, and Lithotabs.

Lithobid: A trade name for the antimanic drug lithium.

Lithotabs: A trade name for the antimanic drug lithium.

lorazepam: A benzodiazepine antianxiety medication. Its trade name is Ativan.

L-tryptophan: The major building block of the neurotransmitter serotonin. L-tryptophan may prove helpful in treating depression.

Ludiomil: The trade name for maprotiline, a four-ring antidepressant thought to be as effective as the tricyclics.

major depression: The affective illness marked by decreased self-esteem, inability to concentrate, and lack of energy. When major depressiom occurs in the setting of past manic episodes, the patient is said to have bipolar disorder.

mania: The "high" phase of affective illness marked by elation, increased energy, increased activity, and, often, decreased judgment.

manic-depressive illness: Affective illness in which episodes of both mania and depression have occurred; bipolar disorder.

MAOI: See *monoamine oxidase inhibitors.*

maprotiline: A four-ring antidepressant thought to be as effective as the tricyclics. Its trade name is Ludiomil.

Marplan: The trade name for the monoamine oxidase inhibitor isocarboxazide.

methylphenidate: A stimulant drug that may be useful for treating depressions in which other medications have failed. Its trade name is Ritalin.

mixed affective disorder: An affective disorder in which symptoms of depression and mania exist simultaneously.

monoamine oxidase inhibitors (MAOIs): Antidepressant medications that work by inhibiting monoamine oxidase, an enzyme that breaks down norepinephrine, serotonin, and other neurotransmitters.

motivated behavior: A behavior, associated with a hungerlike experience, that is somehow "wired" into the body to satisfy a basic biological need. Eating, sleeping, and sexual behaviors are naturally occurring motivated behaviors. Drug dependence and alcohol dependence, on the other hand, are artificially induced by repeated exposure to the substance.

multiple sclerosis: A disease in which the sheathing around neurons degenerates, making rapid impulse transmission impossible and leading to blurred vision, slurred speech, and muscle weakness. Manic and depressive symptoms may also be seen.

Nardil: The trade name for the monoamine oxidase inhibitor phenelzine.

neuroleptic: A medication that helps to relieve psychotic symptoms, such as delusions or hallucinations; synonymous with *antipsychotic.*

neuron: A cell in the nervous system able to conduct impulses and communicate by releasing and receiving chemical messengers (neurotransmitters).

neurotransmitter: A chemical messenger released by neurons. The neurotransmitters norepinephrine and serotonin have been most closely linked to affective illness.

norepinephrine: A catecholamine neurotransmitter thought to be involved in the pathology of affective illness.

Norpramin: A trade name for the generic tricyclic antidepressant desipramine.

nortriptyline: A tricyclic antidepressant. Trade names include Aventyl and Pamelor.

obsession: A thought recognized as one's own but regarded as silly, wrong, or embarrassing. The thought recurs again and again despite the desire to dismiss it from one's mind. Obsessions are frequently seen in the setting of depression.

obsessive-compulsive: Refers to being troubled by significant obsessions or compulsions. Obsessions and compulsions are common in depression, but each may appear independently.

orthostatic: Associated with standing erect. Orthostatic hypotension refers to a drop in blood pressure when one rises from a sitting or lying position. Symptoms include light-headedness, dizziness, and resulting falls.

Pamelor: A trade name for the tricyclic antidepressant nortriptyline.

panic attack: A sudden period of intense fear or discomfort, usually lasting minutes, during which the victim may be short of breath, dizzy, or nauseated. He or she may also experience chest pain, heart palpitations, hot or cold flashes, or muscle cramps. Often there is a sense of impending doom, as if death is imminent. Panic attacks are common in depression, but they may appear independently.

Parkinson's disease: A disease caused by the death of a group of neurons that use the neurotransmitter dopamine. People with Parkinson's disease suffer from movement abnormalities and, often, from depression.

Parnate: The trade name for the monoamine oxidase inhibitor tranylcypromine.

pathological gambling: The inability to resist impulses to gamble even in the face of severe adverse consequences.

pathology: The bodily abnormality found in a disease. An example is the blockage in a blood vessel that leads to stroke.

pathoplastic effect: The shaping of disease symptoms by personality.

PCP (phencyclidine hydrochloride): A dangerous street drug that can cause symptoms of mania.

Pertofrane: A trade name for the tricyclic antidepressant desipramine.

PET: See *positron emission tomography*.

phencyclidine hydrochloride: See *PCP*.

phenelzine: A monoamine oxidase inhibitor. Its trade name is Nardil.

phentolamine: A drug that can reverse the dangerous rise in blood pressure sometimes seen in individuals taking monoamine oxidase inhibitors. The trade name is Regitine.

phenylketonuria (PKU): An inherited disease in which the amino acid phenylalanine, found in food, is not properly broken down. If the illness goes undetected in the newborn, and the buildup of phenylalanine goes unchecked, mental retardation can result.

phobia: An unreasonable fear that is closely related to a particular situation. Fear of crowds is one example. Phobias are frequent companions of atypical depression.

phototherapy: See *bright-light therapy*.

PKU: See *phenylketonuria*.

positron emission tomography (PET): A radiographic scan that can measure body tissue metabolism.

premenstrual syndrome: Irritability, bloating, abdominal pain, and occasional depressive symptoms that occur during the days prior to menstruation. Premenstrual syndrome sometimes becomes "wedded" to full-blown major depressive episodes, particularly atypical depressions.

Presamine: A trade name for the tricyclic antidepressant imipramine.

protriptyline: A tricyclic antidepressant. One trade name is Vivactil.

Prozac: The trade name for fluoxetine, an antidepressant thought to work by blocking the reuptake of the neurotransmitter serotonin into the neurons that have released it.

psychoanalysis: A theory of psychological development as well as a form of psychotherapy. Psychoanalytic psychotherapy seeks to unearth emotional conflicts, which may have arisen as long ago as childhood, as the source of presently occurring mental disturbances. Techniques employed include free association, decoding of dreams, and interpretation of emotions transferred between patient and therapist and vice versa.

psychoanalyst: One who practices psychoanalysis.

psychosis: Implies loss of contact with reality. The term is usually used to describe conditions that include symptoms such as delusions or hallucinations.

psychotherapist: A practitioner of psychotherapy.

psychotherapy: A treatment for psychiatric disorders in which support, reassurance, and reeducation of the patient, rather than medication, form the basis of treatment. Many different techniques are used, including psychoanalysis and cognitive therapy.

rapid cycling: An affective illness in which episodes of mania or depression occur at least four times within a year.

Regitine: The trade name for the antihypertensive phentolamine.

reserpine: A drug used to treat high blood pressure that works by depleting norepinephrine and serotonin stored in neurons. Depression is a common side effect of treatment.

Ritalin: The trade name for methylphenidate, a stimulant drug that may be useful for treating depressions in which other medications have failed.

seasonal affective disorder: An affective illness that seems to recur at a particular time during the year. The term is usually applied to conditions in which depression occurs during fall and winter, when daylight hours are shortest.

sedative: Causing drowsiness.

serotonin: A brain neurotransmitter made from the amino acid tryptophan. Serotonin metabolism may be out of balance in people with affective disorders.

Sinequan: A trade name for the tricyclic antidepressant doxepin.

SK-Pramine: A trade name for the tricyclic antidepressant imipramine.

sleep therapy: A treatment for depression in which the sleep-wake cycle is altered. A patient might, for example, be kept awake during one full night or during specific hours of several nights.

steroids: Cortisol-like chemicals that can cause symptoms of mania or depression when taken as medication.

stroke: Damage to the brain caused by an interruption of its blood supply. Depression often follows.

syndrome: A group of symptoms that occur together and often herald the presence of an underlying disease.

tardive dyskinesia: A disorder typically characterized by repetitive involuntary movements of the face, mouth, and neck. Tardive dyskinesia can be caused by neuroleptic medications.

Tegretol: One trade name for the antiseizure medication carbamazepine.

thyroid: A gland located in the neck. Imbalances of thyroid hormone can mimic affective illness.

Tofranil: A trade name for the tricyclic antidepressant imipramine.

trait: An enduring dimension of personality, such as independence or dependence, that predicts how a person will respond in a variety of situations.

tranylcypromine: A monoamine oxidase inhibitor. Its trade name is Parnate.

trazadone: An antidepressant thought to work by blocking the reuptake of the neurotransmitter serotonin into the neurons that have released it. Its trade name is Desyrel.

Triavil: A combination medication intermixing the tricyclic antidepressant amitriptyline with the antipsychotic perphenazine.

tricyclic antidepressant: Any of several antidepressant drugs that have a three-ring chain as part of their chemical structure.

tyramine: An amino acid found in many foods. Tyramine is normally broken down by monoamine oxidase. In persons treated with monoamine oxidase inhibitors, therefore, it can accumulate, causing a dangerous rise in blood pressure.

unipolar: An affective illness in which only depressive episodes occur.

Valium: One trade name for the benzodiazepine antianxiety medication diazepam.

valproic acid: An antiseizure medication that may also be useful in treating the symptoms of both depression and mania. Its trade name is Depakene.

vital sense: The subjective sense an individual has about the level of his or her physical and mental energy.

Vivactil: The trade name for the tricyclic antidepressant protriptyline.

Xanax: The trade name for the benzodiazepine antianxiety agent alprazolam. Xanax has also been shown to have antidepressant effects.

Additional Reading

Autobiographical Books

Clifford Beers, *A Mind That Found Itself*, University of Pittsburgh Press, Pittsburgh, Penn., 1981 (first published in 1907).

Patty Duke and Kenneth Turan, *Call Me Anna*, Bantam, New York, 1987.

Norman Endler, *Holiday of Darkness*, Wiley, New York, 1982.

Percy Knauth, *A Season in Hell*, Harper & Row, New York, 1975.

Joshua Logan, *Josh*, Delacorte Press, New York, 1976.

Kurt Vonnegut, *The Eden Express*, Holt, Rinehart and Winston, New York, 1975. (Note: Although Vonnegut was diagnosed as having schizophrenia, his own account seems to indicate that he was suffering from an affective disorder.)

Pamphlets

The following pamphlets are published by the National Institute of Mental Health (NIMH):

Depression: What You Need to Know
Helpful Facts about Depressive Disorders

Helping Bereaved Children: A Booklet for School Personnel
National Education Program on Depressive Disorders
Understanding Bereavement Reactions in Adults and Children: A Booklet for Lay People

Single copies are available at no cost from D/ART, NIMH, Room 15-C-05, 5600 Fishers Lane, Rockville, MD 20857.

The following pamphlets are published by the American Psychiatric Association:

Facts about: Depression
Facts about: Manic Depression
Facts about: Teen Suicide
Facts about: Mental Health of the Elderly

Single copies are available at no cost from the American Psychiatric Association, 1400 K Street, N.W., Washington, DC 20005.

Books on General Psychiatry and Mood Disorders

Ronald R. Fieve, *Moodswing*, Bantam Books, New York, 1976.

John H. Griest and James W. Jefferson, *Depression and Its Treatment*, American Psychiatric Press, Washington, D.C., 1984.

Julie T. Johnson, *Hidden Victims: An Eight-Stage Healing Process for Families and Friends of the Mentally Ill*, Doubleday, New York, 1988.

Donald H. McKnew, Leon Cytryn, and Herbert Yahraes, *Why Isn't Johnny Crying? Coping with Depression in Children*, Norton, New York, 1983.

Demitri F. Papolos and Janice Papolos, *Overcoming Depression*, Harper & Row, New York, 1987.

Norman Rosenthal, *Seasons of the Mind*, Bantam Books, New York, 1989.

Mogens Schou, *Lithium Treatment of Manic-Depressive Illnesses: A Practical Guide*, 3d rev. ed., Karger, New York, 1988.

Solomon H. Snyder, *Drugs and the Brain*, Scientific American Books, New York, 1986.

Ann Kaiser Stearns, *Living through Personal Crisis*, Ballantine Books, New York, 1985.

Books Requiring More Knowledge of the Field

Nancy C. Andreasen, *The Broken Brain: The Biological Revolution in Psychiatry*, Harper & Row, New York, 1984.

Robert Burton, *The Anatomy of Melancholy* (first published in 1621), Vintage Books, New York, 1977.

P. R. McHugh and P. R. Slavney, *The Perspectives of Psychiatry*, Johns Hopkins Press, Baltimore, 1986.

P. R. Slavney and P. R. McHugh, *The Polarities of Psychiatry*, Johns Hopkins Press, Baltimore, 1987.

P. C. Whybrow, H. S. Akiskal and W. T. McKinney, *Mood Disorders: Towards a New Psychobiology*, Plenum Press, New York, 1984.

G. Winokur, *Depression: The Facts*, Oxford University Press, New York, 1981.

References

Ablow, Keith. (1985). "On a Psychiatric Ward, Words Like 'Crazy' Lose Their Meaning." *The Evening Sun*, July 10, p. A9.

Akiskal, Hagop S. (1985). "A Proposed Clinical Approach to Chronic and 'Resistant' Depressions: Evaluation and Treatment." *Journal of Clinical Psychiatry*, 46 (10):32–36.

———and McKinney, William T., Jr. (1975). "Overview of Recent Research in Depression." *Archives of General Psychiatry*, 32:285–304.

———and Webb, William L., Jr. (1983). "Affective Disorders: I. Recent Advances in Clinical Conceptualization." *Hospital and Community Psychiatry*, 34:695–702.

———et al. (1980). "Characterological Depressions." *Archives of General Psychiatry* 37:777–783.

American Psychiatric Association. (1980). *Diagnostic and Statistical Manual of Mental Disorders* (3d ed.). Washington, D.C.: American Psychiatric Association.

———. (1987). *Diagnostic and Statistical Manual of Mental Disorders* (3d ed., rev.). Washington, D.C.: American Psychiatric Association.

Anthony, James C., et al. (1985). "Comparison of the Lay Diagnostic Interview Schedule and a Standardized Psychiatric Diagnosis." *Archives of General Psychiatry*, 42:667–675.

Asberg, M., et al. (1971). "Relationship between Plasma Level and Therapeutic Effect of Nortriptyline." *British Medical Journal*, 3:331–334.

Ayd, F. J., and Blackwell, B. (eds.). *Discoveries in Biological Psychiatry*. Philadelphia: Lippincott, 1970.

Baastrup, P., and Schou, M. (1967). "Lithium as a Prophylactic Agent." *Archives of General Psychiatry*, 16:162–172.

———et al. (1970). "Prophylactic Lithium: Double Blind Discontinuation of Lithium in Manic-Depressive and Recurrent Depressive Disorders." *Lancet*, 11:326–330.

Ball, J.R., and Kiloh, L.G. (1959). "A Controlled Trial of Imipramine in Treatment of Depressive States." *British Medical Journal*, 4:1052–1055.

Baron, M., et al. (1987). "Genetic Linkage between X-Chromosome Markers and Bipolar Affective Illness." *Nature*, 326:289–292.

Barraclough, B., et al. (1974). "A Hundred Cases of Suicide: Clinical Aspects." *British Journal of Psychiatry*, 125:355–373.

Bartlett, John. *Familiar Quotations*. Boston: Little, Brown, 1980.

Beck, A. T. (1976). *Cognitive Therapy and the Emotional Disorders*. New York: International Universities Press.

———, Brady, J. P., and Quen, J. M. (1977). "The History of Depression." *Psychiatric Annals*. New York: Insight Communication Inc.

Beers, Clifford. (1981). *A Mind That Found Itself*. Pittsburgh, Penn.: University of Pittsburgh Press.

Behar, D., Winokur, G., and Berg, C. (1984). "Depression in the Abstinent Alcoholic." *American Journal of Psychiatry*, 141:1105–1107.

Biederman, Joseph, et al. (1985). "Depressive Disorders in Relatives of Anorexia Nervosa Patients with and without a Current Episode of Nonbipolar Major Depression." *American Journal of Psychiatry*, 142:1495–1497.

Bloch, S. (1979). "Supportive Psychotherapy." In Bloch, S. (ed.), *An Introduction to the Psychotherapies* (pp. 196–220). New York: Oxford University Press.

Bowen, Rudradeo C., et al. (1984). "Types of Depression in Alcoholic

Patients." *Journal of the Canadian Medical Association*, 130: 869–874.

Burton, Robert. (First published in 1621) (1977). *The Anatomy of Melancholy*. New York: Vintage Books.

Cantwell, Dennis P., et al. (1977). "Anorexia Nervosa: An Affective Disorder?" *Archives of General Psychiatry*, 34:1087–1093.

Carroll, B.J. (1985). "Dexamethasone Suppression Test: A Review of Contemporary Confusion." *Journal of Clinical Psychiatry*, 46(supp. 2):13–24.

Carroll, B.J., et al. (1981). "A Specific Laboratory Test of the Diagnosis of Melancholia." *Archives of General Psychiatry*, 38:15–22.

Checkley, S. A., et al. (1984). "The GH Response to Clonidine in Endogenous as Compared with Reactive Depression." *Psychological Medicine*, 14:773–777.

Coppen, A., et al. (1971). "Prophylactic Lithium in Affective Disorders." *Lancet*, 11:275–279.

Crowe, R.R. (1984). "Electroconvulsive Therapy—A Current Perspective." *New England Journal of Medicine*, 311:163–167.

deFigueiredo, John M., and Frank, Jerome D. (1982). "Subjective Incompetence, the Clinical Hallmark of Demoralization." *Comprehensive Psychiatry*, 23:353–363.

DeMontigny, C., et al. (1983). "Lithium Carbonate Addition in Tricyclic Antidepressant–Resistant Unipolar Depression." *Archives of General Psychiatry*, 40:1327–1334.

DePaulo, J. R. (1984). "Lithium." *Psychiatric Clinics of North America*. 7:587–599.

———. (1986). "Affective Disorders." In Barker, L. Randol, Burton, John R., and Zieve, Philip D. (eds.), *Principles of Ambulatory Medicine* (pp. 183–195). Baltimore: Williams and Wilkins.

———, Correa, E. I., and Sapir, D.C. (1986). "Renal Effects of Lithium: A Longitudinal Study." *American Journal of Psychiatry*, 143:892–895.

———and Simpson, S. G. (1987). "Therapeutic and Genetic Prospects of an Atypical Affective Disorder." *Journal of Clinical Psychopharmacology*, 7:50–54S.

Egeland, J. A., and Sussex, J. (1985). "Suicide and Family Loading for Affective Disorders." *Journal of the American Medical Association*, 254:915–918.

————et al. (1987). "Bipolar Affective Disorders Linked to DNA Markers on Chromosome 11." *Nature*, 325:783–787.

Endicott, J., et al. (1985). "Bipolar II: Combine or Keep Separate?" *Journal of Affective Disorders*, 8:17–28.

"The Experience of Electro-Convulsive Therapy." (1965). *British Journal of Psychiatry*, 111:365–367.

Feighner, J. R., et al. (1972). "Diagnostic Criteria for Use in Psychiatric Research." *Archives of General Psychiatry*, 26:57–63.

Fieve, Ronald R. (1976). *Moodswing*. New York: Bantam.

Folstein, Marshal F., and McHugh, Paul R. (1982). "The Neuropsychiatry of Some Specific Brain Disorders." In Lader, M. H. (ed.), *The Handbook of Psychiatry* (vol. 2, pp. 107–118). Cambridge, Cambridge University Press.

Folstein, Susan E., et al. (1983). "Conduct Disorder and Affective Disorder among the Offspring of Patients with Huntington's Disease." *Psychological Medicine*, 13:45–52.

Frank, Jerome D. (1974). "Psychotherapy: The Restoration of Morale." *American Journal of Psychiatry*, 131:271–274.

————. (1979). "What Is Psychotherapy?" In Bloch, Sidney (ed.), *Introduction to the Psychotherapies* (pp. 1–21). New York: Oxford University Press.

Freeman, C. P. L., and Kendell, R. E. (1980). "ECT: I. Patients' Experiences and Attitudes." *British Journal of Psychiatry*, 137:8–16.

Freud, Sigmund. (1957). "Mourning and Melancholia." In Strachey, James (ed.), *The Standard Edition of the Complete Psychological Works of Sigmund Freud* (vol. 14, pp. 243–258). London: Hogarth Press and the Institute of Psychoanalysis. (Original work published 1917.)

Garfinkel, P.E., Stancer, H.C., and Persad, E. (1980). "A Comparison of Haloperidol, Lithium Carbonate and Their Combination in Treatment of Mania." *Journal of Affective Disorders*, 2:279–288.

Gillin, J.C. (1983). "The Sleep Therapies of Depression." *Progress in Neuro-Psychopharmacology & Biological Psychiatry*, 7:351–364.

———et al. (1981). "Age-Related Changes in Sleep in Depressed and Normal Subjects." *Psychiatry Research*, 4:73–78.

Glassman, A., et al. (1977). "Clinical Implications of Imipramine Levels." *Archives of General Psychiatry*, 34:197–204.

Gold, Mark S., with Morris, Lois B. (1987). *The Good News about Depression*. New York: Villard Books.

Goodwin, Donald. (1986). Book review of *The Perspectives of Psychiatry*. *Journal of Clinical Psychiatry*, 47:480.

Goodwin, F. K., and Bunney, W. E. (1971). "Depressions Following Reserpine: A Reevaluation." *Seminars in Psychiatry*, 3:435–448.

Goodwin, F. K., and Jamison, K. R. "The Natural Course of Manic-Depressive Illness," in Post, R. M. and Ballenger, J. C. (eds.), *The Neurobiology of Mood Disorders*. Baltimore, Williams and Wilkins.

———et al. (1982). "Potentiation of Antidepressant Effects of L-Triiodothyronine in Tricyclic Nonresponders." *American Journal of Psychiatry*, 139:34–38.

Gregory, S., Shawcross, C. R., and Gill, D. (1985). "The Nottingham ECT Study: A Double-Blind Comparison of Bilateral, Unilateral and Simulated ECT in Depressive Illness." *British Journal of Psychiatry*, 146:520–524.

Greist, John H., and Jefferson, James W. (1984). *Depression and Its Treatment*. Washington, D.C.: American Psychiatric Press.

Guze, S., and Robins, E. (1970). "Suicide and Primary Affective Disorders." *British Journal of Psychiatry*, 117:437–438.

Hagnell, Olle, Lanke, Jan and Rorsman, Birgitta. (1981). "Suicide Rates in the Lunby Study: Mental Illness as a Risk Factor for Suicide." *Neuropsychobiology*, 7:248–253.

Hamilton, Max. (1982). "The Effect of Treatment on the Melancholias (Depressions)." *British Journal of Psychiatry*, 140:223–230.

Hasin, Deborah, Endicott, Jean, and Lewis, Collins. (1985). "Alcohol and Drug Abuse in Patients with Affective Syndromes." *Comprehensive Psychiatry*, 26:283–295.

Heninger, G., Charney, D., and Sternberg, D. (1983). "Lithium Carbonate Augmentation of Antidepressant Treatment." *Archives of General Psychiatry*, 40:1335–1342.

Jamison, K., and Winter, R. (1988). *Program Notes and Biographical Notes. Moods and Music*. Washington, D.C.:

Jefferson, J., and Griest, J. (1983). *Lithium Encyclopedia for Clinical Practice*. Washington, D.C.: American Psychiatric Press.

Kaminsky, Michael J. (1986). "Psychotherapy in Patients with Endogenous Depression." Paper presented at The Johns Hopkins School of Medicine Department of Psychiatry and Behavioral Sciences Grand Rounds, Baltimore, The Johns Hopkins Hospital, March 24.

Keller, M. B., et al. (1982). "Recovery in Major Depressive Disorder." *Archives of General Psychiatry*, 39:905–910.

Kraepelin, Emil. (1921). *Manic-Depressive Insanity and Paranoia* (Mary Barclay, trans.). London: Livingstone.

Krauthammer, C., and Klerman, G. (1978). "Secondary Mania: Manic Syndromes Associated with Antecedent Physical Illness or Drugs." *Archives of General Psychiatry*, 35:1333–1339.

Kruger, S. D., Turner, W. J., and Kidd, K. K. (1982). "The Effects of Requisite Assumptions on Linkage Analyses of Manic-Depressive Illness with HLA." *Biological Psychiatry*, 17:1081–1099.

Kuhn, R. (1958). "The Treatment of Depressive States with G22355." *American Journal of Psychiatry*, 115:459–464.

Kupfer, David J., et al. (1981). "REM Sleep, Naps, and Depression." *Psychiatry Research*, 5:195–203.

Lerer, B., et al. (1987). "Carbamazepine versus Lithium in Mania: A Double-Blind Study." *Journal of Clinical Psychiatry*, 48:89–93.

Lewis, A. J. (1971). "States of Depression: Their Clinical and Aetiological differentiation." In *Inquiries in Psychiatry* (pp. 133–140). New York: Science House. Paper originally published in 1938, *British Medical Journal*, ii:875–878.

Lewis, David A., and Smith, Robert E. (1983). "Steroid Induced Psychiatric Syndromes: A Report of 14 Cases and a Review of the Literature." *Journal of Affective Disorders*, 5:319–332.

Liberman, R., and Raskin, D. (1971). "Depression: A Behavioral Formulation." *Archives of General Psychiatry*, 24:515–523.

Lindemann, Erich. (1944). "Symptomatology and Management of Acute Grief." *American Journal of Psychiatry*, 101:101–148.

Linden, Robert D., Pope, Harrison G., Jr., and Jonas, Jeffrey M. (1986). "Pathological Gambling and Major Affective Disorder: Preliminary Findings." *Journal of Clinical Psychiatry*, 47:201–203.

Lipsey, John R., et al. (1984). "Nortriptyline Treatment of Post-Stroke Depression: A Double-Blind Study." *Lancet*, i:297–300.

Mann, J. J., et al. (1986). "Increased Serotonin₂ and B-Adrenergic Receptor Binding in the Frontal Cortices of Suicide Victims." *Archives of General Psychiatry*, 43:954–959.

Marshall, Eliot. (1980). "Psychotherapy Works, but for Whom?" *Science*, 207:506–508.

McHugh, Paul R. (1987). "Psychiatry and Its Scientific Relatives: A Little More Than Kin and Less Than Kind." *Journal of Nervous and Mental Disease*, 175:579–583.

———. (1987). "William Osler and the New Psychiatry." *Annals of Internal Medicine*, 107:914–918.

———and Slavney, Phillip R. (1986). *The Perspectives of Psychiatry*. Baltimore: Johns Hopkins Press.

McKusick, V. A. (1986). *Mendelian Inheritance in Man*. Baltimore: Johns Hopkins Press.

Meyers, Jerome K., et al. (1984). "Six-Month Prevalence of Psychiatric Disorders in Three Communities." *Archives of General Psychiatry*, 41:959–967.

MRC Clinical Psychiatry Committee. (1965). "Clinical Trial of Treatment of Depressive Illness." *British Medical Journal*, i:881–886.

Nelson, C. et al. (1984). "Drug Responsive Symptoms in Melancholia." *Archives of General Psychiatry*, 41:663–668.

———et al. (1984). "Subjective Complaints during Desipramine Treatment." *Archives of General Psychiatry*, 41:55–59.

Osterweis, M., Solomon, F., and Green, M. (eds.). (1984). *Bereavement: Reactions, Consequences, and Care*. Washington, D.C.: National Academy Press.

O'Sullivan, K., et al. (1983). "A Comparison of Alcoholics with and without Coexisting Affective Disorder." *British Journal of Psychiatry*, 143:133–138.

Paykel, E. S., Klerman, G. L. and Prusoff, B. A. (1976). "Personality and Symptom Pattern in Depression." *British Journal of Psychiatry*, 129:327–334.

Pearlson, G., et al. (1989). "D2 Dopamine Receptors Increased in Psychotic, but Not in Nonpsychotic Affective Disorder." Paper presented at International Congress on Schizophrenia Research, San Diego, April 1989.

Post, R. M., et al. (1983). "Prophylactic Efficacy of Carbamazepine in Manic-Depressive Illness." *American Journal of Psychiatry*, 140:1602–1604.

———et al. (1986). "Antidepressant Effects of Carbamazepine." *American Journal of Psychiatry*, 143:29–34.

———Prein, R., Klett, E. M., and Caffey, C. J. (1972). "A Comparison of Lithium Carbonate and Chlorpromazine in the Treatment of Mania." *Archives of General Psychiatry*, 26:146–153.

Prein, R., Klett, E. M., and Caffey, C. J. (1974). "Lithium Prophylaxis in Recurrent Affective Illness." *American Journal of Psychiatry*, 131:198–203.

Rich, Charles L., Young, Deborah, and Fowler, Richard C. (1986). "San Diego Suicide Study." *Archives of General Psychiatry*, 43:577–582.

Robins, Lee N., et al. (1984). "Lifetime Prevalence of Specific Psychiatric Disorders in Three Sites." *Archives of General Psychiatry*, 41:949–958.

Robinson, R. G., Lipsey, J. R., and Price, T. R. (1985). "Diagnosis and Clinical Management of Post-Stroke Depression." *Psychosomatics*, 26:769–778.

———and Szetela, B. (1981). "Mood Change Following Left Hemispheric Brain Injury." *Annals of Neurology*, 9:447–453.

———et al. (1984). "Mood Disorders in Stroke Patients: Importance of Location of Lesion." *Brain*, 107:81–93.

Rosenthal, Norman E., et al. (1984). "Seasonal Affective Disorder: A Description of the Syndrome and Preliminary Findings with Light Therapy." *Archives of General Psychiatry*, 41:72–80.

————et al. (1985). "Antidepressant Effects of Light in Seasonal Affective Disorder." *American Journal of Psychiatry*, 142:163–169.

————et al. (1986). "Seasonal Affective Disorder in Children and Adolescents." *American Journal of Psychiatry*, 143:356–358.

Scheinin, Anne-Grace. (1983). "The Burden of Suicide." *Newsweek*, Feb. 7, p. 13

Schuckit, Marc A. (1986). "Genetic and Clinical Implications of Alcoholism and Affective Disorder." *American Journal of Psychiatry*, 143:140–147.

Seligman, M. (1975). *Helplessness*. San Francisco: Freeman Press.

Shapiro, Sam, et al. (1984). "Utilization of Health and Mental Health Services: Three Epidemiologic Catchment Area Sites." *Archives of General Psychiatry*, 41:971–978.

Shopsin, B., et al. (1975). "Psychoactive Drugs in Mania." *Archives of General Psychiatry*, 32:34–42.

Slavney, Phillip R., and McHugh, Paul R. (1984). "Life Stories and Meaningful Connections: Reflections on a Clinical Method in Psychiatry and Medicine." *Perspectives in Biology and Medicine*, 27:279–288.

————and————. (1985). "The Life Story Method in Psychotherapy and Psychiatric Education: The Development of Confidence." *American Journal of Psychotherapy*, 39:57–67.

————and————. (1987). *The Polarities of Psychiatry*. Baltimore: Johns Hopkins Press.

Snyder, Solomon H. (1986). *Drugs and the Brain*. New York: Scientific American Books.

Squire, Larry R. (1977). "ECT and Memory Loss." *American Journal of Psychiatry*, 139:997–1001.

————et al. (1981). "Retrograde Amnesia and Bilateral Electroconvulsive Therapy." *Archives of General Psychiatry*, 38:89–95.

Stearns, Ann Kaiser. (1985). *Living Through Personal Crisis*. New York: Ballantine.

Stern, Stephen L., and Mendels, J. (1981). "Drug Combinations in the Treatment of Refractory Depression: A Review." *Journal of Clinical Psychiatry*, 42:368–373.

Stoudemire, A., et al. (1986). "The Economic Burden of Depression." *General Hospital Psychiatry*, 8:387–394.

UCLA Neuropsychiatric Institute and UCLA Department of Music. (1985). *Moods & Music*. Produced by Kay Jamison and Robert Winter. Los Angeles: UCLA.

U.S. Department of Health and Human Services, Public Health Service, Alcohol, Drug Abuse, and Mental Health Administration. (1985). *Depression: What We Know*. Washington, D.C.: GPO.

van Bemmel, A. L., and van den Hoofdakker, R. H. (1981). "Maintenance of Therapeutic Effects of Total Sleep Deprivation by Limitation of Subsequent Sleep." *Acta Psychiatria Scandinavia*, 63:453–462.

VanValkenberg, Charles, et al. (1984). "Anxious Depressions: Clinical, Family History, and Naturalistic Outcome—Comparisons with Panic and Major Depressive Disorders." *Journal of Affective Disorders*, 6:67–82.

Veith, R. C., et al. (1982). "Cardiovascular Effects of Tricyclic Antidepressants in Depressed Patients with Chronic Heart Disease." *New England Journal of Medicine*, 306:954–959.

Weissmann, M. M., et al. (1981). "Depressed Outpatients." *Archives of General Psychiatry*, 38:51–55.

West, E., and Dally, P. (1959). "Effects of Iproniazid in Depressive Syndromes." *British Medical Journal*, i:1491–1494.

"What Should We Tell Patients about Their Medicines?" (1981). *Drug and Therapeutics Bulletin*, 19:74.

Whybrow, P. C., Akiskal, H. S., and McKinney, W. T. (1984). *Mood Disorders: Towards a New Psychobiology*. New York: Plenun.

Winokur, G., Clayton, P. J., and Reich, T. (1969). *Manic-Depressive Illness*. St. Louis: Mosby.

Worral, E. P., et al. (1979). "Controlled Studies of the Acute Antidepressant Effects of Lithium." *British Journal of Psychiatry*, 135:255–262.

Ziegler, V. E., et al. (1976). "Nortriptyline Plasma Levels and Therapeutic Response." *Clinical Pharmacology and Therapeutics* 20:458–463.

Zung, William W., and Green, Robert L., Jr. (1974). "Seasonal Variation of Suicide and Depression." *Archives of General Psychiatry*, 30:89–91.

Index

Al